Return To
E

SPARE YOUR PEOPLE!

SPARE YOUR PEOPLE!

RICHARD SWANSON

Bridge Publishing, Inc.
Publishers of
LOGOS • HAVEN • OPEN SCROLL

All Scripture quotations are from the New King James Version of the Bible, © 1979, 1980, 1982 Thomas Nelson, Inc., unless otherwise identified as King James Version (KJV) or Revised Standard Version (RSV). Used by permission.

Spare Your People
© Richard Swanson, 1986
All rights reserved
Printed in the United States of America
ISBN 0-88270-596-2
Library of Congress catalog number 85-073213
Bridge Publishing, Inc.
2500 Hamilton Blvd.
South Plainfield, NJ 07080

Dedication

To Mom and Dad
who were called
home to glory
during the writing
of this book.

Contents

Foreword xi

Part 1: Mercy in the Midst of Judgment
    1. Sodom and Gomorrah 7
    2. Nineveh 17
    3. Israel 23

Part 2: The State of the Nation
    4. Morals 39
    5. Drugged Society 59
    6. Cults and the Occult 67
    7. Greed, Lust and Pride 71

Part 3: Objections to Judgment
    8. A Godly Heritage 89
    9. Ten Righteous 99
    10. Judgment Before the Rapture? 105

Part 4: America's Judgment
    11. Under Judgment 127
    12. Future Judgments 135
    13. Why Judgment? 157
    14. How Soon? 171
    15. What Shall We Do? 175
    16. If Judgment Comes 191
    17. Persecuted Brethren 199
    18. Revival 207

Acknowledgments

I wish to honor those faithful servants whom God employed to make ths book a reality—first and foremost, those front-line saints who undergirded me with much intercessory prayer, as well as those who ministered many helpful words of encouragement:

Lloyd Hildebrand, whom God sent to inspire me to undertake the humanly impossible task of writing this book, and to Lloyd, Susan Spaulding, Cheryl Swanson, Steve Dunham and Bob Oliver for their editorial expertise, along with Ray Bovino and the entire staff at Bridge Publishing.

Thanks again to Cheryl Swanson, my dear sister, for her tireless, incessant typing, and to the computer people, librarians, Christian bookstore employees, and all others who contributed to the success of this endeavor.

Most of all, I wish to honor and give all the glory to my Lord, Savior and Friend, Jesus Christ, who does all things well.

Foreword

Ever since God "created man in His own image" (Gen. 1:27), He has been deeply involved in the affairs of mankind for their good. In spite of Adam and Eve's disobedience in the garden described in Genesis, chapter 3, and their fallen nature having been passed on to all subsequent generations (see Rom. 5:12), God, through His Son Jesus, has graciously provided a means of reconciliation to himself for each one of their descendants, undeserving as they may be.

This book will first examine the Holy Scriptures as a means of comprehending God's merciful attitude and behavior toward those individuals and nations who deserved judgment. I think most of us, myself included, haven't really heard what God has to say about this important subject.

Second, it will investigate the historical records of various cultures, Christian and otherwise, to learn the consequences for those who have turned from "the paths of righteousness" (Ps. 23:3).

Third, this book will correlate the Holy Scriptures with historical records to improve our understanding of God's work in His Church and in the world today.

And, finally, I believe God has a specific word for the United States of America. Catastrophic judgments are coming. And I, by His grace, am an earthen vessel of His, a watchman on a wall. The Lord willing, I will do my best to tell you what I've seen and heard concerning America.

I pray that this book enables each one of us to learn something more of the ways of God. Amen.

> Let the priests, who minister to the Lord,
> weep between the porch and the altar;
> let them say, "Spare Your people, O Lord,
> and do not give Your heritage to reproach,
> that the nations should rule over them.
> Why should they say among the peoples,
> 'Where is there God?' " (Joel 2:17)

PART 1

Mercy in the Midst of Judgment

How could a God of love permit terrorists to brutally kill a defenseless man confined to a wheelchair? Will that same holy and righteous God offer Myron Klinghoffer's murderers an opportunity to repent? And what of the Fidel Castros and the Moammar Khadafys of this world who mercilessly maim, torture and destroy the innocent? And what of a nation that has legalized the slaughter of millions of human beings in the womb? Have they gone too far? Will God visit them with swift and total destruction? Will eternal damnation be their just and final reward? Before drawing our own conclusions let us first examine God's heart in the matter.

God's righteousness would never allow a sinner, no matter how much He loved him, to be in His presence. For this very reason "He drove out the man" (Gen. 3:24) from the garden, thereby preventing Adam and Eve and their descendants *in their sinful condition* from partaking of the tree of life. What was God to do? His prize creation had disobeyed Him. "Through one man's [Adam's] offense judgment came to all men, resulting in condemnation" (Rom. 5:18). Due to His righteousness, will God some day say to the entire human race, "Depart from Me, you cursed, into the everlasting fire prepared for the devil and his angels" (see Matt. 25:41)? No! God has mercifully decided to offer fallen mankind reconciliation to himself through the sacrifice of His own Son upon a cross. "God was in Christ reconciling the world to Himself, not imputing their trespasses to them ... For He made Him who knew no sin to be sin for us, that we might become the righteousness of God in Him" (2 Cor. 5:19, 21). Christ's atoning blood is God's way—the only way—to reconcile sinners and make them righteous. The Bible says, "Without shedding of blood there is no remission" of sins (Heb. 9:22). "For it is the blood that makes atonement for the soul" (Lev. 17:11). "The blood of Jesus Christ His Son cleanses us from all sin" (1 John 1:7).

God's Love

God by His very nature is loving. "For God so loved the world that He gave His only begotten Son, that whoever believes in Him should not perish but have everlasting life" (John 3:16). God approaches us in love. He wants us to know, whether or not we accept it, how much He loves us. "In this is love, not that we loved God, but that He loved us and sent His Son to be the propitiation [payment] for our sins" (1 John 4:10). His love for sinners is beyond measure. *Jesus loves us.* In her song, "His Kind of Love," Marijohn Wilkens said it so beautifully: "It wasn't nails that held Jesus to the cross. It was His love for us that made Him pay the cost." (© 1974 Buckhorn Music Publications, international copyright secured, all rights reserved.)

Repentance

To be reconciled to God, He requires us to repent. Jesus declared, "Unless you repent you will all likewise perish" (Luke 13:3). The Greek word for "repent" (*metanoia*) means "to change one's mind."[1] We change our minds (repent) by agreeing with God that we are sinners (see Rom. 3:23), by asking God to have mercy upon us (see Luke 18:13), and by accepting the Lord Jesus Christ as our savior from sin (see Matt. 1:21).

God cannot force us to repent, "but is longsuffering toward us, not willing that any should perish but that all should come to repentance" (2 Pet. 3:9). According to the apostle Paul, God "desires all men to be saved and to come to the knowledge of the truth" (1 Tim. 2:4). This doesn't mean all will repent and be saved. Jesus stated the fundamental reason why many will not: "Men loved darkness rather than light, because their deeds were evil" (John 3:19). Is this God's fault? Certainly not. God is drawing them, yet they are like those who, prior to stoning the deacon Stephen, were told by him, "You always resist the Holy Spirit" (Acts 7:51).

Free Will and Foreknowledge

God's love and desire for us to repent and be made righteous in Christ do not negate our free will in determining our relationship with Him, nor do they cloud His foreknowledge of what our decision will be (see Isa. 46:10, Ps. 44:21). How does God correlate the two? The Bible does not clearly reveal how man's free will can operate in unison with God's foreknowledge. God does have His secrets (see Deut. 29:29). I have often pondered this mysterious process as I am sure many of you have. And recently, as I fervently prayed for truth in this area, a verse from the book of Psalms came to mind: "Such knowledge is too wonderful for me; It is high, I cannot attain it" (Ps. 139:6). I am now persuaded God would not have you and I wearying ourselves trying to discern something He has chosen not to reveal. Therefore, in the matter of man's free will and God's foreknowledge complementing each other, we can rest in the fact that God is omniscient and that we are limited.

Cities, Nations and Servants

The Bible provides us with concrete information on how, in the past, God has handled various cities and nations who opposed His will and deserved His wrath. Knowing how God has dealt with other nations will enable us to better understand God's plans and purposes for America today. It would also be profitable to observe how God has employed His servants in ministering to wayward societies, and how He has used the circumstances of those societies to accomplish His will in the lives of His servants.

1
Sodom and Gomorrah

The ancient cities of Sodom and Gomorrah and the surrounding communities comprised a fairly large and quite prosperous metropolitan area. In spite of having achieved an affluent standard of living, Sodom and Gomorrah's moral behavior became increasingly degraded. It had fallen into a selfish, hedonistic, "do your own thing" life style. The Bible states that their transgressions amounted to much more than just homosexuality. The sins of Sodom were: "pride, fullness of food, and abundance of idleness, neither did she strengthen the hand of the poor and needy, and they were haughty and committed abomination" (Ezek. 16:49, 50).

Many of the people in and around Sodom, including Lot, his two daughters and his wife, were not homosexuals or lesbians. But as we shall see there was among them an acceptance of homosexuals (Sodomites). *Unger's Bible Dictionary* states: "The Sodomites were not inhabitants of Sodom, nor their descendants, but men consecrated to the unnatural vice of Sodom as a religious rite."[2]

About 1920 B.C. the cities of Sodom and Gomorrah were plundered by invaders: "They took all the goods . . . and all their provisions, and went their way" (Gen. 14:11). Abraham, the Hebrew, known then as Abram, fought against and defeated the invaders to rescue his nephew Lot and his family, who resided in Sodom; in doing so, he restored to Sodom and Gomorrah all the people and goods that had been taken captive. You would have thought the people of these cities would have responded to God's benevolence by changing their way of living. They didn't. Twenty years later the Lord confided in His friend Abraham: "Because the outcry against Sodom and Gomorrah is great, and because their sin is very grievous, I will go down now and see whether they have done altogether according to the outcry against it that has come to Me; and if not, I will know" (Gen. 18:20, 21). The wickedness of these two cities had reached an ugly crescendo. Their life style demanded divine judgment. Yet God, represented by two angels, traveled to Sodom and Gomorrah in hope that the people there would change for the better. *God isn't anxious to judge but desires to show mercy.*

Abraham's prayer. Most people believe that Lot, Abraham's nephew who dwelt in Sodom, was the catalyst for Abraham's earnest intercession for these cities (see Gen. 18:23-33). Abraham had previously rescued Lot, and was deeply concerned about his nephew's well-being. But Abraham's intercession was also prompted by the revelation of God's merciful plan of going to Sodom.

"And Abraham came near and said, 'Would You also destroy the righteous with the wicked?' " (Gen. 18:23). Abraham was obviously stirred by God's threat of wrath which was intrinsically dependent upon the public response to God. Why bother interceding, nephew or no nephew, if judgment was the only available course? Mercy was a possibility; therefore Abraham's intercession was effective. Did the Lord go down to Sodom looking for one million sinners? No, for ten righteous. If God had found at least ten people who turned from their sins, He would have spared the entire community. (See Gen. 18:32.)

Two Angels and Lot. Sodom and Gomorrah, unlike Nineveh, hadn't received any warning of impending doom; unlike Israel, they had heard no call to repentance; yet God, having sent the two angels, granted the people of Sodom and the entire surrounding area an opportunity for repentance. "Now the two angels came to Sodom in the evening" (Gen. 19:1). Lot, who also played an important role in God's relationship to these two cities, greeted the angels upon their arrival at Sodom; divine providence had placed him at the gate of the city. Lot then persuaded the angels not to tarry in the street all night but in his house, where he prepared a feast for them. "Now before they lay down, the men of the city, the men of Sodom, both old and young, all the people from every quarter, surrounded the house" (v. 4). The entire city was there. "And they called to Lot . . . 'Where are the men who came to you tonight? Bring them out to us that we may know them carnally [commit sodomy]' " (v. 5). Remember, God was being represented by these two angels who appeared in the likeness of men. After the people had made known their wicked intentions, Lot went outside the house and tried to reason with his brethren. "Please, my brethren, do not do so wickedly! See now, I have two daughters who have not known a man; please, let me bring them out to you, and you may do to them as you wish; only do nothing to these men, since this is the reason they have come under the shadow of my roof" (Gen. 19:7,8). (Lot risked his life and family as he desperately tried to restrain the mob from doing any evil.) The men of Sodom angrily replied, "Stand back!" Then they said, "This one came in to sojourn, and he keeps acting as a judge; now we will deal worse with you than with them"! (v. 9). The men of Sodom were bent on satisfying their lust. "So they pressed hard against the man Lot, and came near to break down the door. But the men reached out their hands and pulled Lot into the house with them, and shut the door" (v. 9b, 10). Up until this point repentance had been possible, but now it was too late. The two angels "struck the men who were at the doorway of the house with blindness" (v. 11). Certainly one would think the mob, after being afflicted in this way, would have abandoned their godless efforts; but no, their insatiable desires drove them on, "they became weary trying to find the door" (v. 11b). The Scriptures only mention those who were at the door of the house as being blinded; the rest like spectators at a football game gave their wholehearted support. Inside the house, the two angels broke the news to Lot. "We will destroy this place, because the outcry against them has grown great before the face of the Lord, and the Lord has sent us to destroy it" (Gen. 19:13).

When the grace of God is spurned, judgment is the only recourse. "Then the Lord rained brimstone and fire on Sodom and Gomorrah, from the Lord out of the heavens. So He overthrew those cities, all the plain, all the inhabitants of the cities, and what grew on the ground" (Gen. 19:24, 25) thereby "making them an example to those who afterward would live ungodly" (2 Pet. 2:6).

Modern scholars believe these cities were located at the southern end of the Dead Sea in the "Valley of Siddim," an area now covered by water. In New Testament times, the Jewish historian Josephus beheld the ruins of Sodom and Gomorrah and her sister cities, and wrote: "Next to it [the Dead Sea] lies the land of Sodom, once so rich in crops and in the wealth of its cities, but now dust and ashes.... Indeed, there are still marks of the fire from heaven and the outline of five cities to be seen."[3]

Again, God's original intention for sending the angels, as well as having Lot sojourn in Sodom, was to offer the inhabitants an opportunity for repentance. Unfortunately, after they had rejected God's final offer of mercy, the two angels became God's ministers of destruction. If Sodom and Gomorrah had only heeded Lot's words and had treated the angels in a godly fashion, there would have been no reason for God to annihilate those cities or to rescue Lot. There would also not have been any scathing New Testament rancor of these cities (see Jude 1:7). Jesus said, "If the mighty works which were done in you [Capernaum, a city where Jesus ministered] had been done in Sodom, it would have remained until this day" (Matt. 11:23).

Was Lot in the Will of God?

Many Christians are convinced Lot made a mistake by moving to Sodom. However, the Bible doesn't denote any wrongdoing in Lot's choosing to do so. He and Abraham, because of their great substance, inevitably had to part. He had to go somewhere and that particular area appeared to be the best place to go. He beheld the well-watered plain of Jordan, "pitched his tent even as far as Sodom," and eventually settled there (Gen. 13:10,12).

Lot undoubtedly was aware of Sodom's bad reputation, for when he decided to travel in that direction, the Bible declares, "the men of Sodom were exceedingly wicked and sinful against the Lord" (Gen. 13:13). Was it then God's will for Lot to move to Sodom? In the New Testament, Peter speaks of "that righteous man dwelling among them, in seeing and hearing, vexed his righteous soul from day to day with their unlawful deeds" (2 Pet. 2:8 KJV). "Vexed" in the Greek translation means "to be afflicted, tormented, pained."[4] Lot's consistent witness against their wickedness was the grace of God constantly striving to bring the souls of an undeserving multitude to a "godly sorrow" (2 Cor. 7:10). And although the people of Sodom and Gomorrah refused to repent, the Lord, through Lot's ministry, as well as through the two angels, afforded them a chance to do so. On judgment day, their witness shall render without excuse those in Sodom who continued to live in error. If it wasn't God's will for Lot to move to Sodom, then the Lord certainly made the most of Lot's erroneous choice while he was there.

Jesus compared the rescue of Lot from Sodom to that of the end-time Church being delivered from the wrath that is to come upon this world. "But on the day that Lot went out of Sodom it rained fire and brimstone from heaven and destroyed them all. Even so will it be in the day when the Son of Man is revealed" (Luke 17:29, 30). Jesus' comparison identifies Lot as a type of the Church and Sodom as a type of the world.

The strong parallel between Lot and the Church, and Sodom and the world, further verifies that Lot was in God's will while living in Sodom, as well as leaving it when the time came. Peter, in his epistle, confirmed this analogy. When God destroyed Sodom and Gomorrah, He "delivered just Lot, vexed with the filthy conversation of the wicked" (2 Pet. 2:7 KJV). Here, the Greek meaning for "vexed" is "to exhaust by labor or suffering."[5] Lot and the grace of God had been completely worn out. And like Lot who was delivered, we too must vex our righteous souls daily at the filthy deeds of the wicked.

It is true Lot lingered in Sodom when the men were about to destroy the city. Lot's lingering was not necessarily due to selfishly wanting to remain there, but rather due to his concern for the inhabitants of the city, which included two of his daughters and sons-in-law, who, in spite of his warning, didn't want to leave (see Gen. 19:14). They faced a grave peril: the wrath of God. Perhaps Lot contemplated, "As long as I'm here there's still hope for them." Tragically, both daughters and their husbands, along with Lot's wife who looked back after she had left Sodom, perished in judgment (see v. 19). Was Lot to blame? The Bible is mute on this point. It does not implicate Lot's moving to or living in Sodom as the cause of their punishment.

Blatant Sins. Soon after Lot left Sodom, his two remaining daughters enticed him to become drunk with wine. And while Lot was in a drunken stupor, one of his daughters laid down with him, and he unknowingly committed incest with her. The following night his other daughter did the same. Lot's daughters hadn't devised this plan for the purpose of enjoying illicit sex, but to preserve their father's lineage (see Gen. 19:31-35). These blatant sins were not, as some suppose, the culmination of a degraded life style in Sodom. While at Sodom, Lot remained steadfast and true, as he vexed his righteous soul daily at the deeds of the wicked. But when Lot left Sodom, no longer being in the heat of the battle, he relaxed his defense. He removed his helmet, sheathed his sword, let go his shield, and a fiery dart pierced him through (see Eph. 6:16, 17).

What happened to Lot is not uncommon. Unfortunately, it is often after God's servants are greatly used in the work of the Lord that they fall into disobedience. For many years David steadfastly served the Lord winning victory after victory over those who would oppress Israel. But when God gave David rest from his enemies, he committed adultery and murder (see 2 Sam. 7:1; 11).

Noah faithfully labored 120 years building the ark. His endeavor diligently displayed God's longsuffering to his generation (see 1 Pet. 3:20). But after the flood, when life returned to normal, Noah became drunk (see Gen. 9:21).

Samson accomplished the will of God as he single-handedly delivered Israel from the Philistines (see Judg. 13-15). But after God installed Samson as a judge to rule Israel, he committed fornication. "He loved a woman in the valley of Sorek, whose name was Delilah" (Judg. 16:4).

> The victory is won
> but the battle's not o'er,
> Do all to stand
> and stand therefore . . .
> (see Eph. 6:13-17)

I would not minimize Lot's transgression, or David's, Noah's, or Samson's either. David's sin cost him his family's well-being and the baby's life (see 2 Sam. 12:10, 11). Samson's cost him his life (see Judg. 16:29-31). The Old Testament does not mention Lot or Noah in any significant manner after they fell. This would suggest they were no longer active in the work of the Lord because of their disobedience. Noah's son Ham reacted ungodly to his father's drunken nakedness and as a result his son Canaan was cursed. However, Noah's two other sons, Shem and Japheth, responded in a godly fashion toward their father's sinful condition and were blessed (see Gen. 9:22-27). I would consider the offspring of Lot's incest, Moab ["the father of the Moabites"] (Gen. 19:37) and Ben-Ammi ["the father of the people of Ammon"] (v. 38) to be negative consequences of his sin. Although the Lord gave each of them their own land (see Deut. 2:9, 19), their descendants have for the most part fought against Israel down through the centuries (see Judg. 3:28-30; 1 Sam. 14:47).

God's Mercy. Although David committed adultery and murder, the Lord still evaluated David's whole life as one of "integrity of heart and ... uprightness" (1 Kings 9:4). David's sin is not even mentioned in the New Testament. Of course, due to his repentance, God no longer remembered his sin. The same is true for Lot, Noah, Samson and other Old Testament saints. The New Testament depicts David as "a prophet" (Acts 2:30). It characterizes Noah as "a preacher of righteousness" (2 Pet. 2:5), and Lot a "righteous man" (v. 8). Samson's name is honorably inscribed in the New Testament's "great faith chapter," Hebrews 11 (v. 32).

Since God has highly esteemed these not-so-perfect Old Testament saints, it would behoove us to do the same. It is unfortunate that over the centuries Lot, more than any other Bible character, has been the recipient of an exorbitant amount of undeserved criticism. Thank God, the New Testament clearly presents God's view of Lot's situation. We behold a man who was at the right place at the right time with the right attitude. In spite of Lot's possible error in moving to Sodom, and the blatant sins he committed after leaving, perhaps there is no better demonstration of God's mercy than the New Testament portrayal of Lot as the kind of servant God expects us to be.

2
Nineveh

Nimrod, the mighty hunter, constructed Nineveh around 2300 B.C. on the banks of the Tigris river. Nimrod, whose name means "rebel," also established Babylon. In *Unger's Bible Dictionary*, we read: "After the 12th Century B.C. Nineveh became one of the royal residences of Assyria. Sargon II (772-702 B.C.) elevated it as the capital of the Assyrian empire."[6] Nineveh had grown to encompass three other large cities so that it extended eighteen miles to the south and across the river to the west, with suburbs spreading out even further. It was located in what is now northern Iraq.

About the time of the reign of Jeroboam II, King of Israel (787-747 B.C.), "the word of the Lord came to Jonah the second time, saying, 'Arise, go to Nineveh, that great city, and preach to it the message that I tell you.' So Jonah arose and went to Nineveh, according to the word of the Lord. Now Nineveh was an exceedingly great city, a three-day journey in extent. And Jonah began to enter the city on the first day's walk. Then he cried out and said, 'Yet forty days, and Nineveh shall be overthrown!' " (Jonah 3:1-4). For three days the words of Jonah echoed through the streets of the city. There was no verbal call to repentance, no denouncing about their sins (as when Jeremiah warned Israel), no word of hope for the future, nothing except the cry of imminent wrath.

Jonah's preaching was effective. The residents of the city responded quickly to Jonah's message of gloom and doom. "So the people of Nineveh believed God, proclaimed a fast, and put on sackcloth, from the greatest to the least of them" (Jonah 3:5). The Ninevites did not wait for the thirty-ninth day. They did not have an attitude of haughtiness; they did not say, "*If* we repent, God will forgive us." Most people who think that way never do repent.

Repentance is not a long, drawn-out process compounded by much introspection. It is rather an immediate, *sincere* response to the quick and powerful Word of God, which discerns "the thoughts and intents of our heart" (Heb. 4:12). *This* kind of reaction will always produce "fruits worthy of repentance" (Matt. 3:8).

The King's Reaction. "Then word came to the king of Nineveh" (Jonah 3:6). This was a critical stage. The king could have hardened his heart, as so many other rulers have done (Exod. 8:15), and set himself "against the Lord and against His Anointed" (Ps. 2:2). But not this king. "He arose from his throne and laid aside his robe, covered himself with sackcloth and sat in ashes. And he caused it to be proclaimed and published throughout Nineveh by decree of the king and his nobles, saying, 'Let neither man nor beast, herd nor flock, taste anything; do not let them eat, or drink water. But let man and beast be covered with sackcloth, and cry mightily to God; yes, let every one turn from his evil way and from the violence that is in his hands. Who can tell if God will turn and relent, and turn away from His fierce anger, so that we may not perish?' " (Jonah 3:6-9).

The king's positive reaction to the word of the Lord made Nineveh's national repentance possible. It is tragic today that most Americans, and undoubtedly our Supreme Court, would view this as a violation of the separation of church and state. However, President Reagan's declaration of 1983 as the Year of the Bible, along with his continued effort to reinstate prayer in public schools and his vocal opposition to abortion on demand, are steps in the right direction.

The king's proclamation and the entire population's repentance averted the judgment of God. "Then God saw their works, that they turned from their evil way; and God relented from the disaster that He had said He would bring upon them, and He did not do it" (Jonah 3:10).

Why Jonah Preached Judgment

Just suppose no one in Nineveh had repented at Jonah's preaching. Would we conclude he was only sent to pronounce judgment? This would be logical considering there wasn't any verbal offer for repentance given. Let's face it, during Jonah's time, Assyria, a major Middle Eastern power that ruled Israel's northern kingdom, and had been defeated by King Jeroboam exactly as Jonah had prophesied (2 Kings 14:25), was not high on Jonah's list of places he wanted to go. God had originally commissioned Jonah, saying, " 'Arise, go to Nineveh, that great city, and cry out against it; for their wickedness has come up before Me.' But Jonah arose to flee to Tarshish from the presence of the Lord" (Jonah 1:2, 3). Why do you think Jonah went to Tarshish when God said Nineveh? Was it because he didn't care to be the bearer of bad news to Assyria, enemy of Israel? Of course not.

After Nineveh repented and its judgment had been cancelled, Jonah became exceedingly angry. "Ah, Lord, was not this what I said when I was still in my country? Therefore I fled previously to Tarshish; for I know that You are a gracious and merciful God, slow to anger and abundant in lovingkindness, One who relents from doing harm" (Jonah 4:2). Jonah knew God had sent him to Nineveh to mercifully proclaim His Word of judgment, thus providing the city an occasion for repentance.

The only reason Jonah went to Nineveh was to obey God's will after God had miraculously spared his life, not out of any concern for the Ninevites. Jonah obeyed, but only after God had whipped up a "mighty tempest" that imperiled the ship he was sailing on to Tarshish; only after he was thrown overboard to calm the storm; only after "the Lord had prepared a great fish to swallow Jonah" and save him from drowning; and only after God had instructed the fish to vomit Jonah onto dry land. (See Jonah 1:1-17, 2:10.)

Although Jonah experienced God's mercy, he still grated against God for being merciful to the Ninevites. Hadn't he learned anything? Jonah longed for Nineveh's demise. After leaving Nineveh, Jonah camped outside the city and waited for God to annihilate it. (See Jonah 4:1-5.)

God's response. What was God to do? His servant, blinded by prejudice, groped in darkness. The Lord decided to show Jonah through a series of divinely inspired events His compassion and concern for the Ninevites. The Lord prepared a large plant to shade Jonah. "Jonah was very grateful for the plant" (Jonah 4:6). The Lord felt the same way about the Ninevites. "But as morning dawned the next day God prepared a worm, and it so damaged the plant that it withered. And it happened, when the sun arose, that God prepared a vehement east wind; and the sun beat on Jonah's head, so that he grew faint. Then he wished death for himself, and said, 'it is better for me to die than to live' " (vv. 7, 9). The Lord would have suffered the same negative emotions had Nineveh perished.

In order to make sure Jonah was aware of his own sentiments for the withered plant, God asked him, "Is it right for you to be angry about the plant?" To which Jonah replied, "It is right for me to be angry, even to death!" (Jonah 4:9). *The stage was now set for one of God's greatest revelations of His mercy ever given to man.* The Lord likened Jonah's affections for the plant to His own for Nineveh. "You have had pity on the plant for which you have not labored, nor made it grow, which came up in a night and perished in a night. And should not I pity Nineveh, that great city, in which are more than one hundred and twenty thousand persons who cannot discern between their right hand and their left, and also much livestock?" (vv. 10, 11).

This unanswered question ends the book of Jonah. Jonah, being totally overwhelmed by the reality of God's compassion for the Ninevites, could add nothing. When God's servant knows God's heart, it makes a tremendous difference in his attitude towards God's work.

Conclusion. It is comforting to know what great lengths God will traverse to straighten out one of His servants. God was not content to let Jonah go his own way.

Jesus actually compared himself to Jonah going to Nineveh via the belly of a fish. "For as Jonah became a sign to the Ninevites, so also the Son of Man will be to this generation" (Luke 11:30). Jesus also equated His ministry with Jonah's. "They repented at the preaching of Jonah; and indeed a greater than Jonah is here" (v. 32). These illustrations clearly display God's redemptive power even with our mistakes.

3
Israel

There was a strange silence in the land of Israel from the time of Malachi the prophet in 450 B.C. until A.D. 30 when "the word of God came to John the son of Zacharias in the wilderness. And he went into all the region around the Jordan, preaching a baptism of repentance for the remission of sins" (Luke 3:2, 3). God had sent John the Baptist to prepare Israel to meet its Messiah precisely as the prophet Malachi had predicted. "Behold, I send My messenger, and he will prepare the way before Me. And the Lord, whom you seek, will suddenly come to His temple" (Mal. 3:1).

What better opportunity for repentance could God give to Israel or to anyone than to fulfill, before their very eyes, the Old Testament prophecies concerning the Messiah! When Herod demanded of the chief priests and scribes the location of the Messiah's birth, they answered, "In Bethlehem of Judea, for thus it is written by the prophet: 'But you, Bethlehem in the land of Judah, are not the least among the rulers of Judah; for out of you shall come a ruler who will shepherd My people Israel' " (Matt. 2:5, 6).

The angels, shepherds and wise men confirmed what the Scriptures declared. The devout Simeon and the prophetess Anna expected His arrival. But the nation of Israel had to wait another thirty years after Jesus' birth until the day finally dawned when John the Baptist revealed Jesus the Messiah to Israel. "And John bore witness, saying 'I saw the Spirit descending from heaven like a dove, and He remained upon Him. . . . And I have seen and testified that this is the Son of God' " (John 1:32, 34).

Jesus, throughout His three-year public ministry, continued to fulfill prophecy after prophecy proving himself to be the Messiah. In the synagogue He read from the Old Testament, "The Spirit of the Lord is upon Me, because He has anointed Me to preach the gospel to the poor. He has sent Me to heal the brokenhearted, to preach deliverance to the captives and recovery of sight to the blind, to set at liberty those who are oppressed, to preach the acceptable year of the Lord." When He had finished reading, He declared, "Today this Scripture is fulfilled in your hearing" (Luke 4:18, 19, 21).

"He cast out the spirits with a word, and healed all who were sick, that it might be fulfilled which was spoken by Isaiah the prophet, saying: 'He Himself took our infirmities and bore our sicknesses' " (Matt. 8:16, 17).

Division. Jesus, when He was being manifested as the Messiah by His Father, caused a sharp division among the people back then just as He does today. "And there was much murmuring among the people concerning Him. Some said, 'He is good'; others said, 'No, on the contrary, He deceives the people' " (John 7:12). "And all the multitudes were amazed and said,

'Could this be the Son of David [the Messiah]?' But when the Pharisees heard it they said, 'This fellow does not cast out demons except by Beelzebub, the ruler of the demons' " (Matt. 12:23, 24).

Almost all of the Jewish leaders disavowed Jesus as the Messiah. When it was reported to the Pharisees by the officers, who had tried but failed to arrest Jesus, that "no man ever spoke like this Man!" (John 7:46), the Pharisees replied, "Are you also deceived? Have any of the rulers or the Pharisees believed in Him?" (John 7:46-48).

Good leadership is necessary for any organization to function properly, especially the church. If the leaders are out of line, the entire organization will be out of kilter. The responsibility for the spiritual condition of the church rests squarely upon the leadership (1 Pet. 5:1-4; Heb. 13:7).

Israel Rejects Jesus. There arose in Israel an increasing resistance to Jesus being the Messiah. "For a good work we do not stone You, but for blasphemy, and because You, being a Man, make Yourself God" (John 10:33). In retrospect, John wrote about the Jewish nation as a whole dismissing Jesus as their Messiah, "He came to His own, and His own did not receive Him" (John 1:11).

The final episode in Israel's rejection happened as Jesus was riding into Jerusalem on a donkey, fulfilling one of the greatest signs of His Messiahship, "Rejoice greatly, O daughter of Zion! Shout, O daughter of Jerusalem! Behold, your King is coming to you; He is just and having salvation, lowly and riding on a donkey, a colt, the foal of a donkey" (Zech. 9:9). Jesus had reached the top of the Mount of Olives overlooking Jerusalem, and as he approached the place of descent, suddenly "the whole multitude of the disciples began to rejoice and praise God with a loud voice for all the mighty works they had seen, saying: 'Blessed is the King who comes in the name of the Lord! Peace in heaven and glory in the highest!' " (Luke 19:37, 38). The Pharisees, in the midst of this tremendous time of spontaneous praise and worship of the Messiah, said to Jesus; "Teacher, rebuke Your disciples" (v. 39).

Many times Jesus made known what was in a person's heart. Other times He spoke directly to a person's need or situation. Jesus did not describe for us the attitude of these Pharisees. However, the reply Jesus gave them convinces me these Pharisees were so self-righteous, puffed up and determined to have their own way that even God himself would have to bend to their will. Jesus didn't rebuke them or expose their hypocrisy; but in one final attempt, He not only addressed the futility of their request but also the error of their continual denial of Him as the Messiah. He passionately declared: "I tell you that if these should keep silent, the stones would immediately cry out" (Luke 19:40). Would they now join in and worship the King or had they already gone too far? Nothing more is communicated. Jesus rode on towards Jerusalem.

"Now as He drew near, He saw the city and wept over it, saying, 'If you had known, even you, especially in this your day, the things that make for your peace! But now they are hidden from your eyes. For the days will come upon you when your enemies will build an embankment around you, surround you and close you in on every side, and level you, and your children within you, to the ground; and they will not leave in you one stone upon another, because you did not know the time of your visitation" (Luke 19:41-44). This prophecy was fulfilled in A.D. 70 by the Roman legions under the command of Titus, who destroyed the city and massacred the inhabitants.[7]

What a shame! Israel had been presented one of the greatest opportunities for repentance ever given, yet because of pride and unbelief failed to receive it. "But as many as received Him, to them He gave the right to become children of God, even to those who believe in His name" (John 1:12). Israel's rejection of the Messiah cost them their land and led them into a miserable wilderness journey of nearly 2000 years. Technically, it still isn't over even though they are back in their land. Jesus said, "See! Your house is left to you desolate; for I say to you, you shall see Me no more till you say, 'Blessed is He who comes in the name of the Lord!' " (Matt. 23:38, 39). The God of mercy has sovereignly gathered the unbelieving Jews from all over the world back into the land to prepare them to receive by faith Jesus the Messiah. Once again the nation of Israel shall serve the Lord.

Judgment on Israel Broke Jesus' Heart

Contrary to the opinion that God reaps satisfaction while pronouncing or administering judgment, He neither rejoices nor receives glory in this. " 'As I live,' says the Lord God, 'I have no pleasure in the death of the wicked, but that the wicked turn from his way and live' " (Ezek 33:11). Jesus yearned for the disobedient Jews of His day to turn and live. "Oh Jerusalem, Jerusalem, the one who kills the prophets and stones those who are sent to her! How often I wanted to gather your children together, as a hen gathers her chicks under her wings, but you were not willing!" (Matt. 23:37).

It broke Jesus' heart when people rejected Him. Jesus wept profusely over the unbelieving city of Jerusalem as He does today over unbelievers, knowing the consequences, temporal and eternal, of their rejecting Him as the Messiah. Do we weep over the hardened hearts of sinners, desiring they come to Jesus, rather than suffer the pain of endless torment? A disciple should not speak of judgment or hell without tears in his eyes and groanings in his soul. All too often we relate these crucial matters to the unsaved with either obvious judgmental contempt or cool analytical indifference.

Saul of Tarsus. Jesus treated the vehement Saul of Tarsus with mercy, not condemnation. Saul, like the Ninevites, was totally ignorant of any wrongdoing. The Lord apprehended Saul while on his way to Damascus to arrest Christians, saying, " 'Saul, Saul, why are you persecuting Me?' Saul said, 'Who are You, Lord?' And the Lord said, 'I am Jesus, whom you are persecuting. It is hard for you to kick against the goads' " (Acts 9:5). A goad was an eight-foot sharp, pointed instrument used to guide oxen. Only the Lord knew how tough a time Saul was having coping with life underneath that hard exterior. Saul was blinded as a result of his encounter with Jesus and had to be led by others (see Acts 9:1, 2). Fortunately, when Saul arrived at Damascus, the Lord convinced the fearful disciple, Ananias, of Saul's genuine conversion and persuaded Ananias to go and minister to Saul, who would soon become the apostle Paul (see Acts 9:15, 16). We need to be sensitive to the Holy Spirit when confronting any modern-day Saul of

Tarsus. I'm sure our brethren in communist lands could attest to this.

The Samaritan Village. Many times Jesus spoke to His disciples about His main purpose for coming to earth, His death and resurrection, but they did not comprehend it. "Now it came to pass, when the time had come for Him to be received up, that He steadfastly set His face to go to Jerusalem" (Luke 9:51). And for this reason a Samaritan village wouldn't receive Him. Two indignant disciples, James and John, then inquired of Jesus if it would be His will for them to destroy the village. " 'Lord, do you want us to command fire to come down from heaven and consume them, just as Elijah did?' But He turned and rebuked them, and said, 'You do not know what manner of spirit you are of. For the Son of Man did not come to destroy men's lives but to save them' " (vv. 55, 56).

Paul, in his letter to Timothy, described the correct attitude (right kind of spirit) for a disciple, especially when ministering to the unsaved: "And a servant of the Lord must not quarrel but be gentle to *all,* able to teach, patient, in humility correcting those who are in opposition, if God perhaps will grant them repentance, so that they may know the truth, and that they may come to their senses and escape the snare of the devil, having been taken captive by him to do his will" (2 Tim. 2:24-26, emphasis added).

Had the disciples forgotten what manner of men they were before they believed Jesus to be the Messiah? Paul wrote to the church at Ephesus and reminded them of their dreadful condition prior to trusting Christ.

And you He made alive, who were dead in trespasses and sins, in which you once walked according to the course of this world, according to the prince of the power of the air, the spirit who now works in the sons of disobedience, among whom also we all once conducted ourselves in the lusts of our flesh, fulfilling the desires of the flesh and of the mind, and were by nature children of wrath, just as the others. But God, who is rich in mercy, because of His great love with which He loved us, even when we were dead in trespasses, made us alive together with Christ (by grace you have been saved) (Eph. 2:1-4).

Now that we are "saved," "made alive," "born again," our Lord has commissioned us with the same ministry He gave to His first disciples just prior to His ascension into heaven.

Thus it is written, and thus it was necessary for the Christ to suffer and to rise from the dead the third day, and that repentance and remission of sins should be preached in His name to all nations, beginning at Jerusalem. And you are witnesses of these things (Luke 24:46-47).

Go into all the world and preach the gospel to every creature. He who believes and is baptized will be saved; but he who does not believe will be condemned (Mark 16:15, 16).

It is true, God will condemn those who reject His salvation. We must warn men of the consequences as Jesus did, but never wish them damned as did the two disciples who wanted fire from heaven to consume the Samaritan village. We must remember that God's overriding purpose for providing salvation is to save men, not condemn them.

"For God did not send His Son into the world to condemn the world, but that the world through Him might be saved" (John 3:17). "Jesus Christ came into this world to save sinners" (1 Tim. 1:15). It is for this cause God has commissioned us to preach the Gospel.

Over the centuries God has sent His servants to Sodom and Gomorrah, Nineveh, Jerusalem, and to the ends of the earth, to proclaim mercy in the midst of judgment, not condemnation: to preach to the lost the Gospel of salvation, not destruction. Multitudes are waiting to hear the same message today.

Footnotes to Part 1

1. W.E. Vine, *An Expository Dictionary of New Testament Words* (London: Marshall, Morgan & Scott, 1952; Grand Rapids, MI: Zondervan), p. 282.
2. Merril F. Unger, *Unger's Bible Dictionary*, (Chicago, Moody Press, 1966), p. 1035.
3. Josephus, *The Jewish War*, Trans. by G.A. Williamson (Great Britain: Hunt, Barnard & Co. Ltd. 1959), p. 387.
4. *The Analytical Greek Lexicon Revised*, ed. by Harold K. Moulton (Grand Rapids, MI: Zondervan, 1978), p. 23.
5. Ibid.
6. Unger, *Bible Dictionary*, p. 796.
7. Ibid., p. 578.

PART 2
The State of the Nation

I pray that we have gathered some insight into God's dealings with believers and unbelievers and the societies in which they lived, and have gained a clearer perspective from the Scriptures on what became of those individuals and nations, and why. We now need to apply this information to our own lives and the nations in which we live.

America, the land I live in and love, is presently in a sad state of affairs. America's significant moral decline in the past few decades is an accurate barometer of our country's relationship to God. When ungodly attitudes and rebellious behavior tend to dominate a society or individual, it is a clear warning signal that all moral and godly restraint has been cast aside. Israel at one time reached the nadir of this course. "In those days there was no king in Israel; everyone did what was right in his own eyes" (Judg. 17:6).

America's godly heritage is being increasingly demolished and anarchized by the wrecking ball of *secular humanism*, a subtle but vain attempt to camouflage atheistic views. Atheism isn't really a question of whether or not God exists, but rather a question of whether or not a person will have anything to do with God in his or her own life. "The fool has said in his heart, 'There is no God' " (Ps. 14:1).

American society's gradual rejection of "the God of the Bible," combined with ever increasing acceptance of atheistic philosophies, can only lead to this nation's ruin. There is cause for much alarm.

4
Morals

There is no better example of atheism's encroachment on the American society than the general decline of our moral behavior.

Abortion

Prior to the Supreme Court's 1973 landmark decision (Roe v. Wade) to legalize abortion on a national scale, several states had already passed laws to this effect. Since 1973, fifteen million unborn Americans have been sacrificed, at a continually high rate, on the altars of pleasure. The Alan Guttmacher Institute (the research arm of Planned Parenthood) reports that in 1982 alone abortion mills tallied 1.57 million murders. In 1980, 29.5% of all abortions were performed on teenagers, and 77% upon unmarried women of all ages.[1]

Victims of Abortion. In 1971 I went to a free health clinic in California for medical treatment. While there, I was asked, being a male, to participate in a urine analysis pregnancy test to help the clinic determine the test's accuracy. I agreed. I was told I would possibly have to retake the test, so in the meantime I was led by one of the staff to a secluded waiting room where a dozen or so young women sat in total silence. As I waited for further instructions, I curiously inquired of the young girl sitting beside me the reason for her visit to the clinic. To my utter astonishment she responded in a tone of despair: "I'm here to get an abortion." (I later found out that she was only fifteen.) The fear of God struck deep into my heart. I glanced around the room and asked some of the other women seated close by if they too were there to get abortions. A few managed to pronounce an audible yes; others sadly bowed their heads in agreement.

At that time, I had only a shallow relationship with Christ, and little Bible knowledge. But I was able to share with the women how it was God who had given life to each one of us, and that we had no right to end the life of the unborn. I also told them there were plenty of couples waiting to adopt children, so there was no need for an abortion. The result was that the fifteen-year-old decided to carry her baby, while a few of the others said they would consider doing the same. I was then called out of the room by one of the physicians, whom I sensed had lingered until my conversation with the young women had concluded.

God's Word. There are numerous Scriptures that prove human life begins at conception and is preordained by God. God said to Jeremiah: "Before I formed you in the womb I knew you; before you were born I sanctified you; and I ordained you a prophet to the nations" (Jer. 1:5). David commented, "For You have formed my inward parts; You have covered me in my mother's womb . . . My frame was not hidden from You, when I was made in secret . . . Your eyes saw my substance, yet being unformed. And in Your book they all were written, the days fashioned for me, when as yet there were none of them" (Ps. 139:13, 15, 16). I think the best biblical example of human life in the womb is John the Baptist. "And it happened, when Elizabeth heard the greeting of Mary, that the babe leaped in her womb; and Elizabeth was filled with the Holy Spirit" (Luke 1:41). An interesting thought for expecting mothers. Spirit-filled mothers can produce Spirit-filled babies.

The penalty for killing an unborn child in ancient Israel was death. God said to Moses while on Mount Sinai, "If men fight, and hurt a woman with child, so that she gives birth prematurely . . . [and] if any lasting harm follows, then you shall give life for life" (Exod. 21:22, 23).

Sadly enough, in spite of the solid biblical evidence for human life beginning at conception, many denominations in America today have adopted a "pro-choice" stand on abortion, defending the right of the mother to decide whether or not to end the life inside her womb.

Abortion's History. Back in the so-called "primitive" existence of man, parents would sacrifice their infants as burnt offerings to various gods. Besides being an effective method of birth control, the sacrificing of infants to the gods provided the parents, especially the mother, a soothing religious rationale (which is the best kind) for their tormented souls. If today's modern abortion methods had been available, I'm sure the parents would not have waited for the children to be born before killing them.

Ancient Israel also practiced infant sacrifice. "And they built the high places of Baal . . . to cause their sons and their daughters to pass through the fire to Molech [a Moabite god]" (Jer. 32:35). This was a chief reason for God sanctioning the Babylonians' conquest of Jerusalem by the sword, famine and pestilence, and to burn it. (See Jer. 32:28-36). How much longer will God allow America to murder its unborn?

During the zenith of Greek civilization, abortion techniques remained archaic and unreliable; therefore, the exposure of infants (infanticide) was commonly practiced. Over the centuries, infanticide greatly reduced the population of Greece. A few years after the Roman conquest of Greece in 146 B.C., the Greek historian Polybius wrote, "In our time the whole of Greece has been subject to the low birth rate and a general decrease of the population, owing to which cities have become deserted and the land has ceased to yield fruit . . . For as men had fallen into such a state of luxury, avarice, and indolence that they did not wish to marry, or if they married to rear the children born to them, or at the most but one or two of them, so as to leave them in affluence to bring them up to waste their substance—the evil insensibly but rapidly grew. For in cases where of one or two children, the one was carried off by war and the other sickness, it was evident that the houses must have been left empty . . . and by small degrees cities became resourceless and feeble."[2]

Due to improved abortion procedures, infanticide rarely occurred among the rich in Roman society. About 75 A.D., Juvenal, a Roman satirical poet, wrote, "Poor women endure the perils of childbirth, and all the troubles of nursing . . . but how often does a gilded bed harbor a pregnant woman? So great is the skill, so powerful the drugs, of the abortionist!"[3] Historian Will Durant cited "a serious decline of population" in Western Europe as the underlying cause of the collapse of the Roman Empire. The main reason for this decline, wrote Durant, was the widespread practice of "family limitation" (abortion and infanticide).[4]

Divorce

The moral framework of our society cannot sustain over a million divorces annually. The National Center for Health statistics show there was one divorce for every two marriages in 1984. This was a drastic reduction from the one-to-four ratio in 1955. The tragic reality is that 40% of all first marriages in America and 44% of all second marriages will end in divorce.

Liberal divorce laws have unquestionably made divorce an easier option than remaining with one's mate and reconciling differences. California was the first state to legalize "no-fault" divorce. Either party can demand, and, after a series of short court proceedings, be granted what is termed by the California Family Law Act of 1970 a "dissolution of a marriage." No one has to remain married who doesn't want to. Presently, every state except Illinois and South Dakota has some form of no-fault divorce.

America is not the only nation to indulge in prolific no-fault divorce. For most of its duration, the Roman Empire recognized a mere letter to one's spouse, announcing one's intentions, as legal divorce. In Rome, women divorced their husbands as readily as men divorced their wives.[5] No doubt this life style inspired the poet Juvenal to sarcastically quip, "So her conquests grow: eight husbands in five Octobers [years]."[6] Even more descriptive of Rome's matrimonial disorders is the simple epitaph of Quintus Vespillo to his wife: "Seldom do marriages last without divorce until death; but ours continued happily for forty-one years."[7] The empire's continual high divorce rate increased the disruption of family life in each successive generation, ultimately causing the empire's collapse.

The Bible clearly states two conditions for divorce. Jesus mentioned one of the conditions in Matthew 5:32: "But I say to you that whoever divorces his wife for any reason except sexual immorality causes her to commit adultery." The other condition was set forth by the apostle Paul in his epistle to the church at Corinth. "But if the unbeliever [mate] departs, let him depart; a brother or sister is not under bondage in such cases. But God has called us to peace" (1 Cor. 7:15). Sadly, many Christian churches in America today recognize without reservation the divorce of its church members. This view is tantamount to an endorsement of the same no-fault divorce our states have adopted, the result being that Christian divorce, once unheard of, is now commonplace in America.

Effects of Divorce. Divorce is creating a precarious environment in the home, in turn increasing the amount of instability in society. Every year, because of divorce, more and more women are forced to become sole providers for their families, creating a financial dilemma not to mention the disciplinary problems of single-parent households. The U.S. Commission on Civil Rights released a report in April, 1983, which stated that the number of poor families headed by women between 1970 and 1980 had increased by 2.8 million, a whopping 54% increase. In 1960, one in every ten poverty-level homes was headed by women; now the ratio is one in five.

Divorce can be calculated in numbers and in dollars and cents, but the psychological effect it has upon family members, especially children, cannot be measured by mere statistics.

Sexual Immorality

Sexual immorality, which includes adultery, fornication, incest, homosexuality, and other perversions, is the primary cause of the breakdown of the American home. According to the 1980 census, an ever increasing number of men and women, 1.5 million, have elected to live together, ignoring any kind of marriage contract. This number has tripled from a decade ago. The 1983 report of the U.S. Commission on Civil Rights informs us that the number of never-married mothers rose 3.4 million between 1970 and 1980, a jump of 365%!

Several years ago in Portland, Oregon, during a T.V. audience-participation discussion program on unwed teenage mothers, a local pastor, Ron Rohman, made a discerning observation. He said something like this: "I notice there are a number of mothers of unwed teenage mothers present, as well as some of the children of unwed teenagers. The question I would like to ask you, and not only you but all of us here as well, is: *Where are the men?* The response was absolute silence.

The Gay National Task Force, headquartered in New York City, presently estimates about 23 million Americans or 10% of the population is either homosexual or lesbian. The Task Force surmises that 10% of any given population is gay. This statistical generality is insufficient in determining whether America's gay population is increasing, decreasing or remaining stable. However, American Gay Pride Day parades and rallies are no longer confined to New York City and San Francisco, known centers of homosexual acceptance. According to the co-chairman of Gay Pride Day activities in Wichita, Kansas, a Gay Pride Day parade was held in almost every major American city in June of 1984. He estimated there were thirty such parades in all, as well as numerous Gay Pride Day festivals, rallies and other various events celebrating the gay life in smaller cities and towns.

The gay community's increased activity is due to greater numbers, which include new converts as well as former closet homosexuals and lesbians who have recently gone public. Like Sodom and Gomorrah, American society's overall acceptance of homosexuality and lesbianism as alternative lifestyles, as opposed to deviant or sinful ones, has unquestionably helped establish the gay community as part of the American way of life.

The recent disclosure of children being heterosexually and homosexually abused at day-care centers across our nation is only the tip of the iceberg. The American Humane Association noted that 56,667 cases of child molestation and nearly 48,000 cases of incest were reported to child protection agencies in 1982. However, these statistics cannot accurately determine the extent of sexual abuse of children in America because they cover only about 40% of America's child population, and because most incidents go unreported. Dr. Henry Giaretto, psychologist and founder of the Child Sexual Abuse Treatment Program in Santa Clara, California, believes the actual number of sexually abused children is much higher. He estimated that in 1984 alone one million children were sexually violated in America. Dr. Giaretto believes 90 to 95% of these children were victimized either by an adult family member or an older friend.

Statistical surveys have provided a partial picture of the problem. Diana Russel, a sociologist at Mills College in Oakland, California, conducted a random survey of 930 San Francisco women in 1978. The study showed that one in three women had been sexually abused before the age of eighteen. Nearly half of the sexually abused women were victims of an incestuous family relationship. Other surveys have produced comparable data.

Pornography. America's six-billion-dollar-a-year, legal, adult, X-rated, criminal-controlled porno business is no longer confined to sleazy theater districts; it has now spread to many homes via cable T.V. and home video cassettes and discs.

Despite a new tough 1984 federal law prohibiting the use of children under eighteen in pornography, America's illegal kiddie-porn industry continues to prey upon the bodies of countless innocent children each year. The actual number of children involved is unknown. A U.S. General Accounting Office survey of fifteen states revealed that 4,619 children were victims of pornography between 1979 and 1982. Dr. Judianne Densen-Gerber, President of Odyssey Institute, a child advocate group, estimates about 3,000 children nationwide currently participate in pornography.

Law-enforcement agencies have obtained evidence substantiating a large network of "kiddie-porn" film studies and distribution centers operating in New York City, Los Angeles, Houston, New Orleans and other metropolitan areas throughout the United States. The children used in the production of pornographic movies and magazines are either runaways, stolen, enticed by neighbors, relatives or friends, or in some cases sold into this hellish slavery by their parents.

During a seminar exposing the plight of these little ones, Dr. Judianne Densen-Gerber showed pornographic movies of children being subjected to various forms of sexual degradation, and slides of children beaten, burned and even murdered!

Once the children begin to develop into manhood or womanhood, they are routinely discarded by the smut peddlers for younger ones. If they survive this torturous servitude, the exploited children usually graduate to prostitution.

Prostitution has also reached epidemic proportions in America. In 1982, the Criminal Justice Institute estimated there were 450,000 prostitutes in America. It is assumed that 20% to 25%, or 90,000 to 120,000, were teenaged or younger. Estimates vary. Dr. Densen-Gerber surmises that the juvenile prostitute population in America is much higher, approximately 2.4 million. As in child pornography, there is not enough statistical information to accurately determine the number of children who are involved in prostitution.

Most prostitutes have managers (pimps) and, like the children used in pornography, have been manipulated and coerced into living an incarcerated life style. At best, they escape the bondage and are physically and/or emotionally scarred for the rest of their lives. At worst, they are killed.

A Better Life. Not wanting to be late for dinner at a mission, I hurriedly walked past two prostitutes seated on a sidewalk bench, smoking marijuana with their customers. Here were some people created by God for His purposes, yet without Christ their lives were headed for disaster. At the time my mind was on not missing supper at the mission; I had no idea that in the next several minutes someone's life would change forever. After taking several more steps, I prayed, "Lord, you've got to give me something to help them."

Suddenly, as if propelled by some unseen force, I spun around towards the group exclaiming, "Jesus has something better for you than marijuana!" I then proceeded to share the love of Jesus with them. The words just seemed to flow out beautifully. Surely the Holy Spirit graciously used me to make His loving appeal to them. Immediately, one of the girls responded with a glowing countenance reflecting that she was whole-heartedly receiving these words of life. The other girl, seated next to her, unfortunately rejected the message and cursed viciously. The two customers looked on with mocking contempt. I then turned and headed towards the mission, content that God had answered my prayer.

After realizing that Christ had a better life for her than getting loaded and selling her body, Janice* (the girl who reacted favorably to the Gospel) decided to quit her pimp. She was in her early twenties and had no difficulty securing a job as a waitress in a local

---

* Her real name is not used in order to protect her identity.

restaurant. When I went there, I didn't recognize Janice as she waited on me at the counter. Her hands shook violently as she placed a cup and saucer on the counter and then poured the coffee in. She remarked, "I'm not used to this kind of work." I tried to encourage her, saying, "God will help you and give you peace." What really bothered Janice wasn't her inexperience as a waitress but the inevitable reprisal of her ex-pimp who would kill her rather than let her leave. A few days later, while seated at the counter, I saw Janice for the last time. I caught a quick glimpse of her through an open door as she walked across the kitchen area of the restaurant. It finally occurred to me that she was the same girl who, while smoking marijuana on the sidewalk, had gladly received God's good news of salvation. The following day I returned to the restaurant; she wasn't there. A few days passed; no sign of her. Neither the manager nor any of the employees seemed to know what had happened to her.

A few months after my encounter with Janice, the Lord directed me to visit brethren in another state. Several months later I returned and inquired of a local pastor as to Janice's possible whereabouts. This is the story he told me. . . . A girl who had quit her pimp had been savagely beaten, and admitted to the hospital's intensive-care unit for three weeks. After she sufficiently recovered from her injuries, the local authorities helped her to start life over again. They issued her new identification, presented her with a large sum of money, and assisted her in relocating in another area of the country.

Janice's courageous stand for Christ not only benefited her but also resulted in a concerted effort by municipal government, business, churches, and civic organizations to end prostitution's grip upon their city. However, the tragedy was that most of the area's prostitution trade shifted to a nearby city across the river.

Greeks and Romans. When sexual immorality becomes the norm in any society, the family unit will no longer be a stabilizing force. The Greek and Roman empires are prime examples of sexual immorality's debilitating influence. The French historian Mommsen described the effect government-taxed slave prostitution had on the average Roman family: "The ties of family life became relaxed with fearful rapidity. The evil of grisettes [slave girl prostitutes] and boy favorites [used for homoerotic acts] spread like a pestilence."[8]

Although there is no evidence of widespread incest, the abundant child slave population of both Greek and Roman societies was extensively used for prostitution. The madams who managed Greek brothels would purchase slave girls, or claim exposed female infants and rear them in the courtesan trade, thus insuring for themselves a luxurious life style. Demosthenes, a renowned Greek statesman, orator and lawyer, recounted a court case involving one such unfortunate slave girl and her madam: "Neacra was one of seven little girls bought when small children by Nicarete, a freed woman who had been the slave of Charisius of Elis. Nicarete was a clever judge of beauty in little girls, and moreover she understood the art of rearing and training them skillfully having made this her profession from which she drew her livelihood. But after she had reaped her profit from the youth of each of them, one by one, she then sold the whole lot of them together, seven in all."⁹

American children, like Janice, being held hostage by pimps and smut peddlers, are no better off than the child slave prostitutes of ancient Athens and Rome.

Sin Diseases. The sexual behavior of the American people must change if our nation is to survive. Hopefully, as people begin to see the consequences of an illicit sexual life style, they will seek a different way of life.

Venereal disease (VD) dates back to Roman times. Its symptoms are accurately described in the sixth book of the Roman medical journal "De Medicina." The resurgence of VD is no coincidence but a tragic result of America's sex-oriented society. According to data compiled by the Center for Disease Control (CDC) in Atlanta, 879,587 cases of gonorrhea and 69,686 cases of syphilis were reported in 1984. The CDC also estimated that, during this same time period, between 200,000 and 500,000 people contracted genital herpes, an incurable type of VD. Overall, twenty-five million Americans may have been affected, reports the CDC. What makes genital herpes so threatening, as opposed to other kinds of VD, is that it has been proven in a U.C.L.A. laboratory to live outside the body for seven hours on towels, and two hours on toilet seats. Genital herpes can be transmitted by physical contact as well as sexual intercourse. Once infected, the victim has it for life.

New strains of VD have also continued to evolve. The chamydial variety can be transmitted from mother to infant. According to the CDC, one third of all pneumonia cases in infants six months and under can be attributed to chamydial. This disease also has caused an estimated 75,000 cases of an eye infection, conjunctivitus, in children each year.

The AIDS (Acquired Immune Deficiency Syndrome) epidemic we have heard so much about continues to afflict American society. It is also known as the "gay plague" because 73% of the cases reported to the CDC by the end of January 1986 were male homosexuals. The rest included male and female drug addicts who used hypodermic needles, recipients of blood transfusions, children of high-risk parents including those who contracted AIDS while in the womb, and heterosexual contacts (CDC statistics).

AIDS destroys the victim's own natural defense mechanisms and leaves the body vulnerable to all types of disease. The prognosis is not good, the CDC reports—only about 28% of AIDS patients survive three years or more.

The scary aspect of AIDS is that it is now spreading to heterosexuals as well. The drug addicts and blood recipients were infected with the disease through contaminated blood. Pregnancy, the closeness of an infected parent to his or her child, and the intimacy of an infected partner in a heterosexual relationship have also provided sufficient atmosphere for transmission of the disease.

The scientific experts as well as society at large are worried. The number of newly reported AIDS cases in the United States doubled in the ten monhts ending January 1986.

The Bible warns the sexually immoral of far worse consequences than venereal disease or AIDS if they do not repent. "Do not be deceived. Neither fornicators ... nor adulterers, nor homosexuals, nor sodomites ... will inherit the kingdom of God" (1 Cor. 6:9).

"The . . . sexually immoral . . . shall have their part in the lake which burns with fire and brimstone" (Rev. 21:8). In Matthew's gospel, Jesus further defined sexual immorality as an attitude of the heart. "But I say to you that whoever looks at a woman to lust for her has already committed adultery with her in his heart" (Matt. 5:28).

Jeremiah prophesied of Judah's adulterous generation just prior to the Babylonian invasion. " 'They committed adultery and assembled themselves by troops in the harlots' houses. They were like well-fed lusty stallions; every one neighed after his neighbor's wife. Shall I not punish them for these things?' says the Lord. 'And shall I not avenge Myself on such a nation as this?' " (Jer. 5:7-9). The Bible records the attempted sodomy rape of the two angels of God as the last sinful act committed in Sodom and Gommorah prior to their destruction. (See Gen. 19:1-11.)

The Bible explicitly condemns incest. "None of you shall approach anyone who is near of kin to him, to uncover his nakedness: I am the Lord" (Lev. 18:6). The *Matthew Henry Commentary* correlates the approaching to uncover nakedness with the seventh commandment, "You shall not commit adultery" (Deut. 5:18). The Bible lists a number of interfamily relationships in which sexual activity is deemed incestuous. These include: parent and child, grandparent and grandchild, brother and sister, aunt and nephew, uncle and niece; whether by wholeblood, half-blood, or marriage, as well as father and daughter-in-law and brother and sister-in-law (see Lev. 18:6-18). The penalty described in the Bible for incest between consenting adults in ancient Israel except in the case of a "concubine" (Lev. 19:20) was death (see Lev. 20:11, 12, 17, 19-21). There was no penalty for unsuspecting children or unconsenting adults: both parties had to mutually agree (see v. 17).

Conclusion. Throughout our land, sexual immorality has spawned an unprecendented number of divorces, abortions, pornographic magazines and movies, and other social ills. Both Scripture and history concur: any nation or individual that has traveled the road of sexual immorality as far as America has gone has ceased to exist. America's engrossment with sexual immorality is yet another warning signal flashing, "Danger! Do not proceed any further."

New Creation. Is it possible for a sexually immoral person, particularly a homosexual or lesbian, to be delivered from his or her sin and become a new creation in Christ Jesus? Yes! The Bible speaks to those Christians who were once homosexuals, adulterers, and fornicators, as well as thieves, coveters, and drunkards (see 1 Cor. 6:9-10). "And such were some of you. But you were washed, but you were sanctified, but you were justified in the name of the Lord Jesus and by the Spirit of our God" (1 Cor. 6:11).

Cannot we who are sanctified and justified in that same name of Jesus accept these ex-homosexuals, ex-lesbians, and other formerly immoral persons for what they are now—blood-washed brethren—instead of rejecting them for what they once were?

At one time, being ignorant of the Scriptures, I too assumed homosexuals and lesbians to be beyond salvation. But God changed my mind. I had often visited the MUNI (short for municipal), a New York City men's soup kitchen on East Third Street in Manhattan. I went there to share Jesus with the men who would idly sit or stand in the large auditorium waiting for breakfast, lunch or dinner to be served in the basement dining hall. During the winter it was not unusual to see 300 or more men show up for dinner. Nor was it unusual to see a dozen or more homosexuals, many of them in drag (dressed in women's clothing) gathered towards the corner of the auditorium next to the bathroom. For several months I had been witnessing to individuals and to small groups at the MUNI. I avoided the homosexuals. Subconsciously I felt God had given up on them, especially the ones in drag, or those who had undergone sex-change operations (transexuals). But one fateful day, as I was passing by their section at a safe distance, one of them began to loudly declare his views on life. "Hey! There are good bitches [drag queens] and bad bitches. We're just like anybody else. Some of us you can trust; some of us you can't." Then he began to assert moral judgments supporting his and his companions' life style. "Some people drink; others smoke. What's good for some ain't good for others." The further away I moved the less attention I paid to what he was saying. I had shut my ears to his words. But I couldn't help but wonder: "God, do you want me to share the gospel with *them!*"

Before I had even finished thinking the question, the anointing of the Holy Spirit came upon me mightily. I nearly floated over to the homosexuals. I sat down in their midst and began to share Jesus. After a few minutes I was interrupted by a question. "Do you have any cigarettes?" asked a tall slim man dressed in leather. I told him I didn't smoke because Jesus had delivered me from cigarettes. I continued to share the gospel until I was again interrupted by the same man.

"Do you have any rollin' tobacco?" he demanded. "I told you I don't smoke anymore; I just praise the Lord now," I said. Suddenly the man, who was in the beginning stages of becoming a drag queen pimp, lashed out: "I'm tired of this ... [deleted]." Grabbing me around the collar, he pressed his angry face against mine and snorted; "If you don't get up from that chair, I'm gonna kill you." I don't recall what happened next. I was so afraid, I fainted. But as fast as I had lost consciousness, I was now standing on my feet filled with the Spirit, praising the Lord. And this one who had been threatening to take my life was now cowering against the wall like a scared dog in fear of losing his. I began to walk about the auditorium continually praising the Lord.

The following day I was afraid to return to the soup kitchen, thinking, "He didn't kill me yesterday, but if I go back there today he'll kill me for sure." I began to pray as I walked in that direction. The presence of the Lord was with me. I arrived at the MUNI just in time to hear a little four foot, nine inch lady from Brooklyn preaching the gospel as if she were six foot, five. She commanded the attention of the large crowd of men in the auditorium. She concluded her sermon with an altar call. She invited those who desired to accept Jesus as their Savior to come forward and pray. Immediately a tall slim man dressed in leather headed quickly towards her and knelt down at her feet. Was it him? Could this be the same man who, only the day before, had threatened to kill me? After praying, he arose from his knees and with calm resolve walked towards the door I had just entered. It was him.

He noticed me. And as he passed by where I stood, he spoke in a tone of relieved certainty, saying, "I'm never comin' back here again."

5
Drugged Society

Drug addiction, whether it be physical or mental, is no respecter of persons. It makes no difference who you are or what you do; if you "play in its park" you will inevitably lose to this vicious tyrant. Drugs haven't any sympathy for the ignorant or for those depressed by life in general, and least of all for those who are thoroughly convinced they can control their use of drugs through moderation.

Cocaine. The most severe drug problem facing America today isn't heroin, LSD, alcohol or marijuana. It's cocaine. There are four to five million cocaine users in America today, with an estimated 400,000 to one million hard-core addicts spending approximately thirty-five billion dollars annually on 125 tons of powdered euphoria.[10,11] The American dream for these people, who are in many cases highly skilled and educated, has become a hellish nightmare.

Although cocaine doesn't kill as many people as heroin or alcohol, it is extremely physiologically addicting. When someone first begins to use cocaine, it is said they feel like God. But gradually cocaine completely enslaves the user's mind and body while destroying all other interests.

In spite of our government's crackdown on cocaine smuggling, there doesn't appear to be any ebb to the flow of this ugly menace that reaches our shores. Most experts are of the opinion that the current cocaine epidemic in America is going to get worse. Thomas B. Kirkpatrick, Executive Director of the Illinois Drug Commission, believes "the use of cocaine will double in the U.S. before we see any decline in its popularity."[12]

Marijuana. Hard scientific evidence verifies that marijuana is as physically harmful to humans and animals as is tobacco. A 1975 study revealed a weak .8% tetrahydrocannabino (THC)* marijuana cigarette had contained 50% to 100% more of the carcinogens (cancer-producing agents) benzanthracene and benzopyrene than a standard high-tar tobacco cigarette.[13] In 1980, Dr. Gary Huber, Director of the Smoking and Health Research Program of Harvard University, conducted research that showed marijuana accelerated the activity of certain enzymes by 200%, contributing to the "eating" or digesting of the lung itself.

Over the years, a substantial amount of clinical research has conclusively proven marijuana to be detrimental to human and animal blood cells, reproductive cells and cycles, brain cells and waves, nerve cells, and lung and skin tissue.

---

* THC is the principal active ingredient in marijuana; it produces the euphoric effect.

The bad thing about marijuana is that it appears to be so good. No vomiting, hangover, shakes or withdrawal interfere with its intoxicating effect. Marijuana doesn't appear to create the same overpowering physical and psychological addiction upon its users as do heroin or cocaine. This is why more than *twenty million Americans* "turn on" with grass.[14]

The devil seems to operate best under these conditions. One of the quickest ways to open yourself to demonic activity is to smoke pot. *Pharmakos* is the Greek word for someone who uses drugs for spiritual enlightenment. Its root word *pharma* is the same word used to form our word pharmacy. *Pharmakos* is translated in the Bible as "sorcerer" or "wizard." This helps explain the heavy drug influence in the occult. "But the . . . sorcerers . . . shall have their part in the lake which burns with fire and brimstone, which is the second death" (Rev. 21:8).

I smoked marijuana for the last time in 1972. I was standing in front of a stove, smoking a joint, waiting for my peyote tea to boil, when what appeared to be an angel of light entered the kitchen. The being was covered in what seemed to be a garment of whitish-gold strands of luminous light. As he moved closer to where I was standing, he announced: "I am Jesus." There was a noticeable hissing sound in his speech. I discounted this imperfection, and in total amazement marveled, "Wow, it's Jesus!" Suddenly the visible glory of this angelic being overshadowed me. I was literally drenched by the being's presence. I can honestly say I have not been more proud in all my life. I could no longer see this being, but while I was inflated by his proud presence he spoke to me, but this time in a clear non-hissing authoritative voice: "I give you power to become my warlock!" My immediate response to his offer was a definite yet peaceful *no* that welled up from deep within my spirit. The satanic being left.

I had become a Christian several months prior to this experience. True, I was no longer injecting drugs or popping pills, but being unaware of what the Bible said about drug use, and having heard so often that marijuana was a natural, harmless herb created by God, I had compromised my abstinence from intoxicants.

Alcohol. Alcohol was and still is the chief executioner of American citizens. The National Council on Alcoholism estimates that in 1985 about 95,000 people died as a direct or indirect result of alcohol. Approximately 25,000 of these deaths resulted from drunken drivers. Although many states have recently raised their legal drinking age to twenty-one, alcohol-related traffic fatalities are presently the leading cause of death in people between the ages of fifteen and twenty-four.

Alcoholism has cost America's free-enterprise system billions of dollars annually in lost wages, and for treatment and prevention programs. A 1983 case study published by the Congressional Office of Technology Assessment calculated the current annual cost of alcohol misuse in America at $120 billion. And what of the untold heartache, misery and pain alcohol has caused the 23 million alcoholics and their loved ones and friends in this country alone? Meanwhile, the domestic wholesale liquor industry netted a hefty $37 billion in sales for 1984.[15]

The Scriptures warn us of the evils of alcoholism. "Who has woe? Who has sorrow? Who has contentions?

Who has complaints? Who has wounds without cause? Who has redness of eyes? Those who linger long at the wine, those who go in search of mixed wine. Do not look on the wine when it is red, when it sparkles in the cup, when it swirls around smoothly; at the last it bites like a serpent, and stings like a viper. Your eyes will see strange things, and your heart will utter perverse things. Yes, you will be like one who lies down in the midst of the sea, or like one who lies at the top of the mast, saying: 'They have struck me, but I was not hurt; they have beaten me, but I did not feel it. When shall I awake, that I may seek another drink?' " (Prov. 23:29-35). "Wine is a mocker, intoxicating drink arouses brawling, and whoever is led astray by it is not wise" (Prov. 20:1). "Do you not know that the unrighteous will not inherit the kingdom of God? Do not be deceived. Neither . . . [will] drunkards . . . inherit the kingdom of God" (1 Cor. 6:9, 10).

On a national scale, God sarcastically informed the alcoholic populace of Israel's southern kingdom of the coming of the foreign conquerors: "Awake, you drunkards, and weep; and wail, all you drinkers of wine, because of the new wine, for it has been cut off from your mouth. For a nation has come up against My land" (Joel 1:5).

Most Americans are keenly aware of the pitfalls of alcohol and drugs, yet why have so many turned to them? Have they given up? Do they really believe they can control their use while receiving the enjoyment they give? The answers to these questions lie in the fact that human beings are gullible, as was Eve in the garden (see Gen. 3:6), and therefore prone to magnify the seemingly beneficial attributes of things so diabolically evil. On the other hand, some people rush into disobedience with their eyes wide open, as did Adam in the garden (see Gen. 2:16, 17 and 1 Tim. 2:14).

Satan's Tool. The place is Ft. Lauderdale, Florida. The time is the vacation period between the spring and fall semesters of most American colleges and universities, better known as the "spring break." Next to the beach front, along the main thoroughfare A1A, a large circus tent filled with games, prizes, amusements and plenty of beer is open for business. Placed near the entrance to the area, a 40-foot-high polyurethane Budweiser beer bottle towers above the earth. Outdoor loudspeakers, amplifying the sound of fun and frolic inside, beckon others to enter. On A1A, a four-wheeled 14-foot-long Miller High Life beer bottle cruises by. It passes paid hucksters who give away free Budwiser, Schaefer, or Miller High Life t-shirts, caps and other advertisement paraphernalia. Overhead a seemingly unending drone of planes is pulling long wavy banners that advertise all the local night clubs, as well as the brand names of alcoholic beverages. Cold beer is being sold everywhere, even in gas stations.

The above scene literally describes what myriads of young people from all over the globe are exposed to every year during spring break. Day after day my soul became increasingly troubled as I beheld the young people woefully led astray by this unabashed glorification of alcohol. Then the Holy Spirit revealed to me how Satan, the deceiver, was using alcohol as a tool to keep young people from turning to Jesus, and to draw young people away from Him.

Satan, our adversary, just doesn't walk up to somebody and say, "Hi, I'm the devil. I don't want you to give your life to Jesus" or, "I want you to stop serving Jesus." The enemy approaches us in many deceptive and subtle ways, and one of those ways, contrary to popular opinion, is **a** bottle of beer.

6
Cults and the Occult

Another disturbing element that is adversely affecting our society, especially the young, is the growing number of Americans involved in cults or occultic practices.

Walter Martin, a leading authority on cults, stated in his book *Rise of the Cults*[16]:

> A cult, then, is a group of people polarized around someone's interpretation of the Bible and is characterized by major deviations from orthodox Christianity relative to the Christian faith, particularly the fact that God became man in Jesus Christ.

From McDowell and Stewart's book *Understanding the Occult*[17] we learn: The word "occult" comes from the Latin word *occultus* and it carries the idea of things hidden, secret and mysterious. Hoover lists three characteristics of the occult:

1. The occult deals with things secret or hidden.
2. The occult deals with operations or events which seem to depend on human powers that go beyond the five senses.
3. The occult deals with the supernatural, the presence of angelic or demonic forces.

Satan is never at a loss when it comes to figuring out new schemes to deceive mankind. The adherents of certain cults, the Mormons for example, and certain occult practioners such as psychics, identify themselves as Christian. Members of other cults such as Hare Krishna and those involved in yoga will state that what they do and believe is in line with the teachings of Christ. No matter what they say, Satan is still the head of all cults and occultic activity.

"Satan . . . transforms himself into an angel of light" (2 Cor. 11:14); therefore his true identity may not be associated with a particular cult or occult practice, or even known by those who are in leadership. That is why those who participate in occult activity and those who are members of or are associated with a cult are genuinely convinced that they have received something from God. On the other side of the coin, Satan has actually gone as far as to persuade his worshipers that he will ultimately be victorious over Jesus, and will then rule and reign throughout eternity. I believe this to be the same lie Satan employed to induce a number of the angels to follow him in his rebellion against God (see Rev. 12:7-9).

The greatest lie Satan has perpetrated on mankind is that the human spirit is divine. Eastern religions such as Hinduism, Buddhism, and Taoism are convinced that Christ or the "Godhead" already dwells within all human hearts, as well as in every living thing. It naturally follows that people who think this way won't believe they need Jesus to save them from their sins, or need to be born again by the Spirt of the living God, if they already have divinity inherent within themselves. If you happen to be one of those who lay claim to some sort of divinity, this verse is for you: "If therefore the light that is in you is darkness, how great is that darkness!" (Matt. 6:23).

I am grieved to think of the lives that are being squandered in Satan's folly. Several years ago, the Jehovah's Witnesses filled a large sports stadium for their annual week-long series of meetings. Every year they gather in a different city. I saw all these nice families, well groomed and mannered. They appeared as gentle lambs at the mercy of ravenous wolves. I asked the Lord, "Why are these who look so pure and godly caught up in something so diabolical and satanic?" Then, as I looked into the face of one of the clean-cut husbands, his eyes became as those of a blind man, with no color in his pupils—*stone blind.* I then realized these were those "whose minds the god of this age has blinded, who do not believe, lest the light of the gospel of the glory of Christ, who is the image of God, should shine on them" (2 Cor. 4:4).

The 3.5-million-member Mormon Church (the Church of Jesus Christ of Latter-day Saints) is the largest cult in America today. Jehovah's Witnesses are second with 600,000 members. In his book *The Cult Explosion*,[18] Dave Hunt estimated the number of cults in America to be around 5,000. Some of the better-known cults include The Way International, the

Worldwide Church of God, the Unification Church, and Scientology. There are also millions of other Americans who dabble in the occult. Some of the more popular occult practices are using ouija boards or tarot cards, fortune telling, palm reading, astrology, witchcraft, seances, and using crystal balls. To this list we could add much more.

If the apostle Paul were to walk the streets of America today, he would undoubtedly have the same reaction as when he trod the avenues of Athens: "His spirit was provoked within him when he saw that the city was given over to idols" (Acts 17:16).

American's entanglement in false religion is another alarm sounding the demise of this nation. Isaiah prophesied against the Israelites for trusting in specific cult and occultic practices to guide them. "Stand now with your enchantments and the multitude of your sorceries, in which you have labored from your youth—perhaps you will be able to profit, perhaps you will prevail. You are wearied in the multitude of your counsels; let now the astrologers, the stargazers, and the monthly prognosticators stand up and save you from these things that shall come upon you. Behold, they shall be as stubble" (Isa. 47:12-14).

The rationale God gave for taking Israel out of the land and sending them to Babylon was, "Just as you have forsaken Me and served foreign gods in your land, so you shall serve aliens in a land that is not yours" (Jer. 5:19).

Every nation and individual would do well to heed the first commandment God gave to Israel: "You shall have no other gods before Me" (Exod. 20:3).

7
Greed, Lust and Pride

I have already discussed some of the more obvious factors that have contributed to the moral breakdown of American society, such as secular humanism, divorce, drug and alcohol addiction, and sexual perversion. But greed, lust and pride—carnal desires that originate in the heart of man—are immorality's strongest abetting force. They will compel a person to devote his or her time, talents, and resources to self instead of to God. Excessive television, sports, and working for monetary gain, as well as gambling, adultery, and drunkenness are examples of their control over the will of a man or nation. America's insatiable appetite for pleasure and material wealth is ample proof of our bondage to these inordinate desires.

Greed

"For the love of money is a root of all kinds of evil" (1 Tim. 6:10).

Greed will motivate a person to methodically smuggle kilos of heroin or cocaine, knowing full well the misery, pain, and death it will cause its recipients. Greed also can placate one's conscience so as not to think of the irreparable damage inflicted on the children he or she has used in filming pornographic movies.

Greed's consequences are not always manifested immediately. Our federal government's current debt of more than two trillion dollars is largely a result of decades of greediness in politics and society. After years of excessive illegal dumping of toxic chemical wastes for profit, America's polluted natural resources are yet another example of greed's prolonged effect upon our culture.

Greed can also take on an air of righteousness. We don't care to think of greed as sin, so we dream up all sorts of nice-sounding cliches such as: "keeping up with the Jones's," "living the good life," or "the American way." The American people are constantly being pressured through television, movies, books and other media to covet—to have something they don't have or to be someone they're not. In spite of the propaganda and phony facade being projected by our free-enterprise system, the Bible says to America today, as it once said to Israel of old, "Thou shalt not covet" (Exod. 20:17 KJV).

Israel. The prophet Amos pronounced God's judgment upon the pleasure-loving, materialistic Israelites who would "sell the righteous for silver, and the poor for a pair of sandals" (Amos 2:6). "Woe to you who are at ease in Zion, and trust in Mount Samaria . . . Who lie on beds of ivory, stretch out on your couches, eat lambs from the flock and calves from the midst of the stall; who chant to the sound of stringed instruments, and invent for yourselves musical instruments like David; who drink wine from bowls, and anoint yourselves with the best ointments, but are not grieved for the affliction of Joseph. [Joseph, one of Jacob's twelve sons, was sold into slavery by his brothers who were covetous of his position with their father and with God.] Therefore they shall now go captive as the first of the captives, and those who recline at banquets shall be removed" (Amos 6:1, 4-7).

It was not sinful for the nation of Israel to possess an abundance of material goods. God judged them because in their wanton desire to become rich they had acquired their wealth at the expense of others, and had subsequently lavished it upon themselves. The love of money—and not money itself—led Israel astray.

The Church isn't immune from greed. In American Christianity today, as in Paul's day, there are "men of corrupt minds and destitute of the truth, who suppose that godliness is a means of gain" (1 Tim. 6:5). Paul's advice to young Timothy concerning those who wrongly equated material prosperity with spiritual success was, "From such withdraw yourself" (v. 5b).

Paul somberly warned Timothy of the dangers of materialistic bondage: "But those who desire to be rich fall into temptation and a snare, and into many foolish and harmful lusts which drown men in destruction and perdition. For the love of money is a root of all kinds of evil, for which some have strayed from the faith in their greediness, and pierced themselves through with many sorrows. But you, O man of God, flee these things and pursue righteousness, godliness, faith, love, patience, gentleness. Fight the good fight of faith, lay hold of eternal life, to which you were also called" (1 Tim. 6:9-12).

Stewardship. Paul instructed Timothy to teach the more materially prosperous brethren the principle of good stewardship. "Command those who are rich in this present age not to be haughty, nor to trust in uncertain riches but in the living God, who gives us richly all things to enjoy. Let them do good, that they be rich in good works, ready to give, willing to share, storing up for themselves a good foundation for the time to come, that they may lay hold on eternal life" (1 Tim 6:17-19).

The Bible does not say you have to be poor to be holy, or rich to be righteous. What God is really concerned about, regardless of how little or how many material possessions we have, is our stewardship. Are we using God's provision to glorify ourselves or Him? The widow's mite (Luke 21:1-4), the parable of the talents (Matt. 25:14-30), the rich young ruler (Matt. 19:16-24), the rich fool (Luke 12:16-21), a brother in need (James 2:14-17), and the good Samaritan (Luke 10:30-37) are all similar illustrations demonstrating the importance of good stewardship.

Prosperity. The Bible mentions a substantial number of believers, such as the apostle Paul (see 1 Cor. 4:9), the begger Lazarus (see Luke 16:19-31), the widow who gave all she had, what little there was (see Luke 21:1-4), and the financially destitute brethren of the great faith chapter Hebrews 11, all of whom were blessed by God yet lacked material luxuries. The Bible also refers to a good many believers, particularly in the Old Testament, who were both spiritually and materially prosperous. These included Job (see Job 42:12-17) and Abraham (see Gen. 13:2) as well as the rich New Testament saints whom Paul had instructed Timothy to counsel.

Real Christian prosperity, like stewardship, is not dependent upon how many or how few material possessions one has. But as the apostle Paul taught Timothy, "Godliness with contentment is great gain" (1 Tim. 6:6). However, our contentment, as well as our faithfulness, is contingent upon how we manage our possessions.

It is our heavenly Father's will that we escape the snare of covetousness and enjoy His prosperity. Therefore, I implore you to make certain your purse strings, along with the other areas of your life, are in the Lord's hands.

Lust

We commonly think of lust as an immoral sexual desire that is associated with various forms of deviant sexual behavior such as adultery, fornication, and homosexuality. However, a person can also lust after many nonsexual items such as drugs, alcohol, nicotine, caffeine or sugar. We can lust after seemingly good things as well. For instance, someone who simply cannot forego watching a particular television program, or playing a certain sport, or eating a favorite food, may be lusting after that thing.

America's supposedly sophisticated culture has helped create a climate conducive to lust. We are repeatedly told to grab all the "gusto" we can; to "go for it" until there is nothing left to go for. This type of free-wheeling, high-rolling hedonistic influence is largely responsible for America's annual $35 billion cocaine habit, $44 billion gambling expenditure, and $30 billion liquor sales, as well as 1.5 million abortions and 1 million divorces.

When America or any nation or individual looses

its ties from the moorings of moral restraint, it can little endure the voluptuous sea of lust. Indulgent Rome and promiscuous Greece have long since vanished beneath its waves and America is sinking fast.

Israel. Lust is wanting something other than what God has given. God miraculously fed Israel manna from heaven in the wilderness (see Exod. 16:4). However, they were not satisfied. They lusted after meat. "Give us meat, that we may eat," they whined (Num. 11:13). The Lord granted their request. He literally showered the surrounding area with a large quantity of quail (see v. 31). "But while the meat was still between their teeth, before it was chewed, the wrath of the Lord was aroused against the people, and the Lord struck the people with a very great plague. So he [Moses] called the name of that place Kirbroth Hattaavah [Graves of Craving], because they buried the people who had yielded to craving" (vv. 33, 34).

After God had established Israel in the land of Canaan, "she lusted for her lovers, the neighboring Assyrians, who were clothed in purple, captains and rulers, all of them desirable young men, horsemen riding on horses. Thus she committed her harlotry with them. . . . With all their idols, she defiled herself" (Ezek. 23:5-7). Therefore, God gave Israel over as captives to those for whom she had lusted (see Ezek. 23). I fear that American society desires the atheistic ways of the Soviet Union rather than the ways of God.

The Church. What happened to the Israelites in the wilderness and later on after God brought them into their land "became our examples," said the apostle Paul, "to the intent that we should not lust after evil things as they also lusted" (1 Cor. 10:6). Lust will render a Christian unclean and unfit for service. For this reason Paul, in his second letter to Timothy, strongly urged him to "flee . . . youthful lusts" (2 Tim. 2:22). Paul's letter to Timothy also connected the consequences of yearning for riches with those of lust. "But those who desire to be rich fall into temptation and a snare, and into many foolish and harmful lusts which drown men in destruction and perdition" (1 Tim. 6:9). Likewise, Jesus warned that "the desires for other things . . . choke the word, and it becomes unfruitful" in our lives (Mark 4:19).

Lust will also terminate the single most important aspect of a Christian's relationship with God: prayer life. The apostle James wrote in his general epistle to the Jewish believers who were scattered because of persecution: "Where do wars and fights come from among you? Do they not come from your desires for pleasure that war in your members? You lust and do not have . . . You fight and war. Yet you do not have because you do not ask" (James 4:1, 2). James further informed them that when they did pray, they prayed selfishly, only asking what they wanted regardless of God's will. "You ask and do not receive, because you ask amiss, that you may spend it on your pleasures" (v. 3).

Are you and I truly praying to know to do God's will, or are we, like the first-century believers James sternly rebuked, merely using God as a spiritual bellhop, demanding He fulfill our every desire? If we are guilty of the kind of prayer life James referred to as spiritual adultery ("friendship with the world" v. 4), then we must do as those early believers hopefully did: repent! Otherwise, James adamantly declared, "Whoever therefore wants to be a friend of the world makes himself an enemy of God" (v. 4).

Pride

The initial sin of Lucifer was pride. "For you have said in your heart: 'I will ascend into heaven, I will exalt my throne above the stars of God; I will also sit on the mount of the congregation on the farthest sides of the north; I will ascend above the heights of the clouds, I will be like the Most High' " (Isa. 14:13, 14).

Pride is the most common of transgressions. Eve, our mother, listened to Satan's spiced, tempting words, "Your eyes will be opened, and you will be like God" (Gen. 3:5). Consequently, both she and her husband did eat of the tree of knowledge of good and evil. Here we see pride at the root of Satan's ability to deceive, and at the root of man's vulnerability to be deceived.

Israel. Israel always ran into trouble when it lifted itself up and no longer depended on the Most High. Just prior to God bringing Israel into the land of Canaan, Moses warned the people, "Beware that you do not forget the Lord your God by not keeping His commandments, His judgments and His statutes which I command you today, lest—when you have eaten and are full, and have built beautiful houses and dwell in them; and when your herds and your flocks multiply, and your silver and your gold are multiplied, and all that you have is multiplied; when your heart is lifted up, and you forget the Lord your God who brought you out of the land of Egypt, from the house of bondage . . . you say in your heart, 'My power and the might of my hand have gained me this wealth' " (Deut. 8:11-14, 17).

Israel's pride brought about its seventy-year Babylonian captivity. Amos cried out to Israel's southern kingdom, whose capital was Jerusalem, "The Lord God has sworn by Himself, the Lord God of hosts says: 'I abhor the pride of Jacob, and hate his palaces; therefore I will deliver up the city and all that is in it' " (Amos 6:8). Over a century later the prophet Jeremiah pleaded in vain with the same two southern tribes. "Hear and give ear: do not be proud, for the Lord has spoken. Give glory to the Lord your God before He causes darkness, and before your feet stumble on the dark mountains, and while you are looking for light, He turns it into the shadow of death and makes it dense darkness. But if you will not hear it, my soul will weep in secret for your pride; my eyes will weep bitterly and run down with tears, because the Lord's flock has been taken captive" (Jer. 13:15-17).

The Church. According to the apostle Paul, much of the sectarianism and strife at the church in Corinth resulted from believers being "puffed up" (proud) (1 Cor. 4:6) over the various gifted Christians who ministered to them (see 1 Cor. 1:10-13). This is also true to a large extent in American Christianity today, except instead of saying: " 'I am of Paul' or 'I am of Apollos' " (1 Cor. 1:12), you and I say "I am of _____." Fill in the blank. Paul's response to the Corinthians' spiritual arrogance would also apply to the church in America today. "Who then is Paul, and who is Apollos, but ministers through whom you believed, as the Lord gave to each one? I planted, Apollos watered, but God gave the increase. So then neither he who plants is anything, nor he who waters, but God who gives the increase" (1 Cor. 3:5-7).

When Christians glorify themselves or each other instead of Christ, when Christians are caught up in an outward show of competitive spirituality rather than being conformed to the image of God's Son, they open the floodgates of sin. The apostle James cautioned believers, "For where envy and self-seeking exist, confusion and every evil thing will be there" (James 3:16).

Paul also lashed out at the Corinthians, who, instead of mourning over the incestuous relationship of one of their members, were once again "puffed up" (1 Cor. 5:2). Because of pride they allowed the guilty party to remain in their midst. The church acted as if nothing was wrong. The Corinthians were too busy "measuring themselves by themselves, and comparing themselves among themselves" to confront sin. (2 Cor. 10:12). Although our sin may not be incest, the same problem that plagued the Corinthian church can affect our individual lives and corporate church life. Pride will deceive a Christian, rendering him content to live with known sin. It will lull him or her into a false sense of security. Paul chided the Corinthian church, "Your glorying is not good. Do you not know that a little leaven leavens the whole lump? . . . Therefore, put away from yourselves that wicked person" (1 Cor. 5:6, 13). Fortunately, after reading Paul's stern letter, the Corinthians humbled themselves, acknowledged their error, and took the necessary steps to correct it (see 2 Cor. 7:8-12). As a result, the man whom the Corinthian believers ejected from their fellowship repented and was subsequently reinstated. (See 2 Cor. 2:6-8.)

Wherever pride reigns, greed, lust and other sins are sure to follow. This is why proud men and nations refuse to admit wrong thinking or action, do not accept criticism or advice, strive to accomplish what is best for them, regardless of the cost or who might suffer, and exhibit words and deeds of kindness, but only as a means of achieving their own goals. Like a blind man walking towards a cliff, a proud man will justify himself with terms such as, "I'm doing my own thing" or "This is right for me." And when events turn sour he takes solace in the rationale, "I did it my way." This kind of person or nation is doomed to failure. Three thousand years ago King Solomon stated in the book of Proverbs: "Pride goes before destruction, and a haughty spirit before a fall" (Prov. 16:18). (See also Prov. 16:5, 18:12, 29:23.) It was no coincidence that God placed "pride" at the top of the list of Sodom's sins.

History has revealed that any nation or individual who has been engrossed in this type of life style and has not repented and forsaken it has inevitably been overthrown by God. Pompous Rome, the French aristocracy prior to the French revolution, Napoleon, Nazi Germany, Communist rulers, Satan himself; all of these and many more like them have been or shall be abased. It matters not how long or how hard they try or have tried to vaunt themselves; sooner or later their kingdoms are reduced to dust.

Have we as a nation—more importantly, have we as the Body of Christ in America—humbled ourselves under the almighty hand of God? Or do we proudly and vainly exalt ourselves? "God resists the proud, but gives grace to the humble" (James 4:6).

Summary

I hope that by having reviewed some of the immoral activities and tainted attitudes to which our nation, Christians included, is in bondage; and by having observed the history of those who have gone the way that we now go; and by having recounted the Biblical warnings of judgment against those who have done what we now do; we would be motivated to a soberness of mind, realizing the great and present danger in which our nation finds itself.

Footnotes to Part 2

1. U.S. Department of Health and Human Services.
2. Polybius XXXVI, 17.
3. Juvenal, *Satires*, VI, 593-6.
4. Will Durant, *Caesar and Christ*, The Story of Civilization, Part III (New York: Simon and Schuster, 1944), p. 665-6.
5. Ibid., p. 134-5.
6. Juvenal, *Satires*, VI, 228.
7. Durant, *Caesar and Christ*, p. 370.
8. Theodore Mommsen, *History of Rome* (New York: Charles Scribner Sons, 1958) vol. 2, p. 483.
9. Demosthenes, 59:18-20.
10. The National Institute on Drug Abuse, Population Projections, 1984.
11. Kurt Anderson, "Crashing on Cocaine," *Time Magazine*, April 11, 1983, p. 23.
12. Anderson, "Cocaine," p. 23.
13. The Saturday Evening Post, September 1980.
14. The National Institute on Drug Abuse.
15. U.S. Bureau of the Census.
16. Walter Martin, *Rise of the Cults* (Santa Anna, CA: Vision House, 1980), p. 12.
17. Josh McDowell & Don Steward, *Understanding the Occult* (San Bernardino, CA: Here's Life Publishers, 1982), p. 9.
    Quoting David H. Hoover, *How to Respond to the Occult* (St. Louis: Concorida, 1979), p. 8. Used by permission.
18. Dave Hunt, *The Cult Explosion* (Eugene, OR: Harvest House, 1980), p. 18.

PART 3
Objections to Judgment

People don't like to hear, talk or think about judgment, particularly when it pertains to them. They rationalize, justify and do all they can do to dismiss any possibility of their doing enough wrong to deserve punishment. Thinking he was unjustly condemned, the thief on the cross tried to escape the penalty for his crime by pleading with Jesus, "If You are the Christ, save Yourself and us" (Luke 23:39).

Whole nations have exonerated themselves beyond reproach. "The backsliding Israel hath justified herself more than treacherous Judah" (Jer. 3:11 KJV). When God confronted the church at Laodicea with divine judgment, the deluded church thought all was well. "Because you say, 'I am rich, and have become wealthy, and have need of nothing'—and do not know that you are wretched, miserable, poor, blind and naked" (Rev. 3:17).

We Americans, Christians included, have also developed a smug arrogance, strongly rejecting any notion of committing sufficient evil to merit God's venting His anger upon our hallowed ground. I shall try to present alternative arguments to those who are convinced God won't judge America—at least not before the Rapture of the Church or the Great Tribulation.

8
A Godly Heritage

Doesn't America's godly heritage prevent God from dispatching any major judgments, such as an invasion of foreign troops, or famine and plague, upon our nation? Nineveh, as we studied earlier, repented in sackcloth and ashes at the preaching of Jonah. God recognized the Ninevites' sincerity and withheld His judgment.

The Ninevites repented in approximately 750 B.C. One hundred years later, the prophet Nahum prophesied: "And it shall come to pass that all who look upon you will flee from you, and say, 'Nineveh is laid waste!' " (Nah. 3:7). He called Nineveh a "bloody city . . . full of lies and robbery" and described her as "the wellfavoured harlot, the mistress of witchcrafts" (vv. 1, 4 KJV).

It is difficult to fathom how Nineveh, after such a thorough repentance, could have fallen so far so fast. God even extended His mercy another thirty-eight years, hoping the inhabitants' memories and Nahum's alarming words would motivate them to repentance, but they didn't. According to *Unger's Bible Dictionary,* "An alliance of Medes, Babylonians, and Scythians destroyed Nineveh in August 1612 B.C., after a two-month siege."[1] We dare not rest upon our godly heritage, expecting God to pass over the flagrant sins of our day.

Antioch

America, unlike Nineveh, has a Christian heritage. Surely this would cause God to be more merciful towards us. However, the city of Antioch was also inhabited by a vibrant evangelical missionary-minded church. The gospel was first preached in Antioch by disciples who had fled the Jewish persecution in Jerusalem. "And a great number believed and turned to the Lord" (Acts 11:21). Barnabas brought Saul (the future apostle Paul) to Antioch. "So it was that for a whole year they assembled with the church and taught a great many people" (v. 26). Then one day the Holy Spirit said to the church at Antioch, "Now separate to Me Barnabas and Saul for the work to which I have called them" (Acts 13:2). The church obeyed and sent them out. In Antioch the disciples were first called Christians (Acts 11:26).

The church at Antioch, in spite of severe persecution, continued to mature and by the benevolent reigns of Diocletian (A.D. 284-305) and Constantine (A.D. 306-337) had developed into one of the most influential Christian churches of that era.

Antioch, "Queen of the East," with a population of half a million, was the third-largest city in the Roman Empire. This prominent city of vast wealth and splendor had another side to it. Antioch became a playground for Rome's military personnel and gained a reputation for shocking sexual behavior.

A great earthquake rocked Antioch in A.D. 526. A quarter of a million people perished. A little over one hundred years later, it was conquered by the Saracens, and then by the Turks in 1084. Since 1268, Antioch has gradually declined under Mohammedan rule. Today it has a population of 6,000.

What happened to Antioch, seedbed of Christianity's missionary movement? Excavation of the ancient city has revealed a number of large church buildings, including Constantine's famous fourth-century octagonal one. Commonly called the "Golden House," the church sported a gilded dome that could be viewed from anywhere in the city. Historian Glanville Downey wrote, "The church itself was constructed of rich marble and the interior was decorated with mosaics, statues, and lamps of silver and bronze."[2] The original Eucharistic vessels which had been confiscated when pagan Emperor Julian closed the church were replaced with golden ones. Another church, elaborately designed in the shape of a cross, dated back to A.D. 367, and the Martyrion at the seaport of Antioch in the fifth century was adorned with magnificent mosaics of wildlife.

History has an awesome way of unsettling one's values and priorities. Possessing this kind of hindsight will often tempt you to close your eyes as you look ahead. The church at Antioch isn't the only church that has seemingly dropped off the face of the earth.

Seven Churches

The book of Revelation addresses seven churches that existed in the eastern half of what is now Turkey.

They too have vanished. Moslem control for the past ten centuries has managed to shut out the Gospel, or is it that God hasn't chosen to reopen that region to the Gospel?

In Paul's day, eastern Turkey was an important logistical part of the world. It connected East with West, Asia Minor with Europe, thereby enabling the area to become the world's leading trade center. And by the sixth century, the Byzantine Empire, as it was then called, became even more prosperous than did the Roman Empire during its height.

The apostle Paul concentrated much of his missionary effort in this area. All three of his journeys and his voyage to Rome touched this part of the world. He sojourned for over two years at Ephesus, nurturing the young church. When in prison, Paul wrote two letters to Timothy exhorting him in his ministry to the local church leaders at Ephesus. Paul also wrote to the church at Colossae and directed them to share their letter with the church at Laodicea. Each one of the seven churches received a prophetic word from God through the apostle John in the book of Revelation (see Rev. 2-3). John the apostle also sojourned at Ephesus, and, due to their proximity, undoubtedly visited the other churches described in Revelation. The famous Nicene Creed was formulated by a church council held in A.D. 325 in the city of Nicaea.

How could a land so saturated with the Gospel become so spiritually parched? I dare say that no history book could adequately elucidate this phenomenon.

We could, to some extent, investigate the reasons why these seven once flourishing churches, along with their influence, have virtually disappeared, but our sources are limited. Therefore, we need to examine more recent Christian cultures where adequate information is available so we may discover from the past where other Christian churches have gone wrong.

Christianity in Russia

The Russian Orthodox Church achieved a material splendor second to none. By the sixteenth century the Orthodox clergy had acquired one third of Russia, a fact generally agreed upon by most modern historians. One million peasants resided on church lands. The church built huge, elaborately furnished churches and monasteries, while the peasants lived in servitude and austere poverty. It is no wonder that in 1762 Peter III ordered all land belonging to churches and monasteries to be incorporated into state properties.[3] Prior to this takeover, the state-appointed "Most Holy All-Ruling Synod" had assumed full responsibility for administering the Russian churches.

They should have listened to Jesus. "Do not lay up for yourselves treasures on earth . . . where thieves break in and steal; but lay up for yourselves treasures in heaven . . . where thieves do not break in and steal. For where your treasure is, there your heart will be also" (Matt. 6:19-21).

The Russian Orthodox Church immersed itself in tradition rather than moving in the power of the Holy Spirit. The liturgy, sacraments, and religious customs were all important. Every home had its icon corner. The dictionary definition of an icon is "a representation in painting, enamel, etc., of some sacred personage as Christ, or a saint or angel, itself venerated as sacred."[4] The church sanctioned the worship of icons, believing they contained miraculous powers. Fairs, carnivals and other secular celebrations which incorporated various rituals, such as the blessing of the Moscow river during Christmas, became the focal point of Christian holidays in Russian society.

The Standists (Baptists) were the only organized church in Russia to study the Bible in worship services. In 1894, they were considered by the state as being especially harmful and forbidden to assemble.

Christianity in Russia prior to 1917 was a sad commentary on how a church drifted away from the reality of the living Christ. The results of this error can still be felt in Russia.

Today, the church in Russia, which includes many born-again believers in the Russian Orthodox Church, is alive and well. I asked Bill Burkett, missionary to the communist lands, what we American Christians could learn from our Soviet brethren. He said, "In those countries they have so little and do so much with so little. Here we have so much and we do so little with so much."

Richard Wurmbrand, who was confined in Rumanian communist prisons for nearly fourteen years for his faith in Christ, describes the Christian church in Rumania prior to the communist takeover in 1945 as lackadaisical, caught up in the routine affairs of denominational life. But when communism took over, Wurmbrand realized, "the second devil was worse than the first." Today, the church in Rumania is also thriving. In Wurmbrand's newsletter, "The Voice of the Martyrs," it is reported that the Rumanian church contains the largest number of Pentecostal Christians of any Eastern Bloc Communist nation.

Norman Allensworth, Scotts Valley Director of the Los Angeles Mission Witness, was a missionary in China at the time Mao came to power. In a letter, he described the Christian church in China as not alarmed by the onslaught of communism. Church life was business as usual until it became too late. Allensworth paralleled the church's situation in China to that of the church in America today.

Summary. When a nation, church or individual departs from the living God, it can no longer depend upon its godly heritage to deliver itself from judgment. The Lord informed Ezekiel that the righteousnes of their forefathers would not save the inhabitants of Israel's Southern Kingdom from being punished for their present disobedience.

> "Son of man, when a land sins against Me by persistent unfaithfulness, I will stretch out My hand against it; I will cut off its supply of bread, send famine on it, and cut off man and beast from it. Though these three men, Noah, Daniel, and Job, were in it, they would deliver only themselves by their righteousness," says the Lord God (Ezek. 14:13, 14).

If those three great American evangelists, D.L. Moody, Charles Finney and Jonathan Edwards, were alive today they too would deliver only themselves, not our nation. The American people, led by Christians, must return to the godly heritage established by our founding fathers; otherwise America will fall.

The Role of the Church

Before continuing the discussion on objections to judgment, I believe it important to emphasize from Scripture the church's role in hastening or preventing God's judgment upon a nation. The church has a direct effect upon the nations for good or evil. When I say "church," I mean born-again believers from whatever denomination. There is only one Church.

Jesus said, "You are the salt of the earth; but if the salt loses its flavor, how shall it be seasoned? It is then good for nothing but to be thrown out and trampled under foot by men" (Matt. 5:13). The warning is plain. Jesus continued, "You are the light of the world. A city that is set on a hill cannot be hidden. Nor do they light a lamp and put it under a basket, but on a lampstand, and it gives light to all who are in the house" (Matt. 5:14, 15). There is a choice to be made here: to shine or not to shine. The decision we make will greatly affect those who are already in darkness. "Let your light so shine before men, that they may see your good works and glorify your Father in heaven" (v. 16).

Paul exhorted the Philippians to become "blameless and harmless, children of God without fault in the midst of a crooked and perverse generation, among whom you shine as lights in the world, holding fast the word of life" (Phil. 2:15, 16).

The best witness is love. Jesus told His disciples, "A new commandment I give to you, that you love one another; as I have loved you, that you also love one another" (John 13:34). Jesus' new commandment wasn't just for the sake of Christian fellowship, but for evangelism as well. "By this all will know that you are My disciples, if you have love for one another" (v. 35).

When we Christians love one another, Jesus is manifested through His Church to the world. Without love, our fellowship is broken. Our light turns to darkness and our salt loses its flavor.

The Church has often been at least partly responsible for civilization falling into the ditch. But when entire hemispheres have landed on skid row, there hasn't been on the face of this earth any better cure for the ills of mankind than the Church of the living God. Nations have come and gone while the Church, though now almost nonexistent in some areas where it once thrived, remains and continues to have a viable influence on the lives of men today.

9
Ten Righteous

The Scriptures tell us God would have spared Sodom if it had contained even ten righteous. Many Americans, especially Christians, are convinced God wouldn't judge America before the Rapture for the same reason. But there is nothing magical about the number ten.

The same case could have been stated for the twelve disciples living in Israel when Jesus pronounced judgment upon Jerusalem and all of Israel as well. Of course, Jesus knew that of the twelve disciples He chose, one of them was a devil. But that still left a total greater than ten.

Let's focus our attention on the town of Capernaum. Today, at the entrance to the ruins of this ancient place, you will read this inscription: Capernaum, the Town of Jesus.

At the beginning of His public ministry, Jesus left Nazareth and moved to Capernaum (Luke 4:29-31). During His three-year public ministry, Jesus spent more time in Capernaum than anywhere else.

The Scriptures refer to Capernaum as "His own city" (Matt. 9:1). Both Peter and Matthew (Levi) resided in Capernaum as well (Matt. 8:14; Mark 2:13). The Bible lists an impressive array of miracles performed by Jesus in Capernaum: the man healed of palsy (Mark 2:11), an unclean spirit cast out (Luke 4:35), the centurion's servant healed (Luke 7:10), the woman with an issue of blood healed (Matt. 9:22, Jairus' daughter raised from the dead (v. 25), and Peter's mother-in-law healed (Matt. 8:15).

There were unquestionably more than ten righteous people living in Capernaum. Why then did Jesus speak the following words of judgment? "And thou, Capernaum, which art exalted unto heaven, shalt be brought down to hell" (Matt. 11:23 KJV). (Not all the people of Capernaum in Jesus' day went to hell; the righteous didn't. But all the residents who rejected Jesus as the Messiah did.)

One day a great crowd gathered at Capernaum, not only to observe, but to receive healing from Jesus. "He cast out the spirits with a word, and healed all who were sick" (Matt. 8:16). Jesus decided after the miracle service to leave Capernaum by boat. "Then a certain scribe came and said to Him, 'Teacher, I will follow You wherever You go.' " (Matt. 8:19). He sounded zealous. Jesus replied, "Foxes have holes and birds of the air have nests, but the Son of Man has nowhere to lay His head" (v. 20). Nothing more was heard from that individual. "Then another of His disciples said to Him, 'Lord, let me first go and bury my father.' But Jesus said to him, 'Follow Me, and let the dead bury their own dead' " (vv. 21, 22). After this, Jesus dismissed the throng and He and His twelve disciples got into a boat and departed for Gadara across the

Sea of Galilee from Capernaum. In Mark's gospel it says, "There were also with him other little ships" (Mark 4:36 KJV).

On the way to the country of the Gadarenes Jesus calmed a storm (Mark 4:37-41). When He arrived He cast out the legion of devils (Mark 5:1-17). Jesus then fed the 5,000, after which He returned to Capernaum in secret because "they were about to come and take Him by force to make Him king" (John 6:15). They didn't realize Jesus' kingdom is not of this world. The people also returned to Capernaum seeking Jesus, not because they saw the miracles, but because they "ate of the loaves and were filled" (John 6:26). They were part of the "what's in it for me?" crowd.

Jesus began to speak in the synagogue at Capernaum to what must have been by now an enormous crowd. He declared himself to be the bread of heaven and required them to eat His flesh and drink His blood (John 6:48-58). His disciples responded, "This is a hard saying; who can understand it?" (v. 60). Jesus then explained the spiritual reality of His previous statement, " 'Does this offend you? What then if you should see the Son of Man ascend where He was before? It is the Spirit who gives life; the flesh profits nothing. The words that I speak to you are spirit, and they are life. But there are some of you who do not believe.' . . . From that time many of His disciples went back and walked no more with Him" (vv. 61-64, 66).

The residents of Capernaum heard the word, saw and received the miracles and were exposed to the ministry of God's Spirit through His Son. For a time they appeared to be (or may very well have been) His disciples. Yet because of "Satan . . . tribulation or persecution ... the cares of this world, the deceitfulness of riches, and the desires for other things" (Mark 4:15, 17, 19) failed to count the cost of not forsaking all for Jesus' sake (Luke 14:28). This is why Capernaum today lies in ruins.

The Righteous and the Wicked

Most American Christians are under the impression God will preserve our national sovereignty because of the vast numbers of believers who dwell in the land. To prove their opinion they generally refer to Abraham's question to God, "Would You also destroy the righteous with the wicked?" (Gen. 18:23). They conclude that God wouldn't judge America for this reason. Most of us have misunderstood what God and Abraham were actually talking about. They weren't merely conversing on whether or not Sodom should be physically destroyed. They were discussing eternal damnation.

It is impossible, as far as eternal judgment is concerned, for the righteous to be destroyed with the wicked. Jesus clearly taught this in many of His parables, including the parable of the wheat and the tares, in which He said to the reapers, "First gather together the tares [wicked] and bind them in bundles to burn them, but gather the wheat [righteous] into my barn" (Matt. 13:30). Also, in the parable of the sheep and the goats, Jesus declared, "And these [wicked goats] will go away into everlasting punishment, but the righteous [sheep] into eternal life" (Matt. 25:46). On the other hand, there are, as in the time of Joshua and Caleb, national judgments in which the righteous will suffer for their righteousness while the wicked simultaneously are punished for their sins.

Israel in the Wilderness

While the nation of Israel camped along the banks of the river Jordan, Moses sent out twelve spies, one from each tribe, to investigate the land beyond the Jordan that the Lord had promised to them. Joshua and Caleb brought back a good report to Israel and encouraged the people to enter the land (Num. 13:30). The ten other spies gave an evil report: "We are not able to go up against the people, for they are stronger than we" (Num. 13:31). The nation of Israel believed the evil report and had to wander in the wilderness under the judgment of God for forty years. Joshua and Caleb and all those under twenty years of age, even though they were innocent of rebelling against God, had to wander along with the rest of Israel.

Why couldn't God have allowed those who believed to enter the land right away instead of condemning them also to wander for those forty years? God could have brought them in quickly, but chose not to. God treated the nation of Israel as one man. He brought them out of Egypt not in stages but as a whole nation. And He determined to bring them into the land of Canaan the same way. But first He had to overthrow in the wilderness those who, in spite of having experienced the miracle of the Red Sea, no longer believed in Him (Jude 1:5; Heb. 3:16, 17; 1 Cor. 10:5). Also, the Israelites under twenty were not mature enough for leadership. Joshua and Caleb, the only ones over twenty who finally entered the Promised Land after leaving Egypt, would have needed the assistance of the older men to possess and inhabit the land. The younger men required more time to physically and spiritually develop.

They suffered together in the wilderness, some for doing good, others for doing evil. Likewise, during Israel's seventy-year Babylonian captivity, righteous Israeli youth, such as Daniel and the three Hebrew boys Hannaniah (Shadrach), Mishael (Meshach), and Azariah (Abed-Nego) were undeservedly carried off to Babylon, suffering the same fate as their disobedient brethren (Dan. 1:3-6). Anyone who lives in this world is going to suffer at some point. Peter noted, "For it is better, if it is the will of God, to suffer for doing good than for doing evil" (1 Pet. 3:17).

The suffering caused by natural disasters such as earthquakes, floods, tornados and hurricanes, along with suffering caused by man-made disasters such as war, industrial accidents and chemical dumping, affects the righteous as well as the wicked. Ever since Cain slew his brother Abel (see Gen. 5:8), both the righteous and the wicked have experienced the suffering produced by physical death. But, thank God, the day is coming when the righteous shall suffer no more.

10
Judgment Before the Rapture?

There has been much worldwide debate over the nuclear arms race. We've heard all about nuclear freeze, Mutual Assured Destruction (MAD), first-strike capability, and more. In spite of all the talk, the threat of nuclear war looms ominously over our planet. Civilization cowers beneath it, permeated by a foreboding sense of hopeless doom. Ever since Hiroshima and Nagasaki, the thought of nuclear holocaust, like a dull toothache, continually reminds mankind of the immense suffering he is capable of inflicting on his fellow man.

The Christian perspective should be much brighter. Jesus said, "And you will hear of wars and rumors of wars. See that you are not troubled; for all these things must come to pass, but the end is not yet" (Matt. 24:6). Believers are not supposed to fret over the threat of war, even nuclear war. Jesus has called us to be *prayer warriors, not war worriers.* Relax—Jesus told us these things would happen. He warned His people in advance, to spare us anxiety. The only time a believer should worry about anything is when he or she is out of the will of God.

In *The Vision* David Wilkerson was deeply troubled over the terrible threat of nuclear destruction facing our world. The Holy Spirit comforted him, saying, "God has everything under control."[5] Jesus went on to say, "For nation will rise against nation, and kingdom against kingdom. And there will be famines, pestilence and earthquakes in various places" (Matt. 24:7). "All these," because of mankind's disobedience, not because of God's will, "are the beginning of sorrows" for the world but not for the Christian who is faithful (v. 8).

The Old Testament prophets and the book of Revelation depict future cataclysmic events strikingly similar to nuclear war. "Their flesh shall dissolve while they stand on their feet, their eyes shall dissolve in their sockets, and their tongues shall dissolve in their mouths" (Zech. 14:12). "The first angel sounded: And hail and fire followed, mingled with blood, and they were thrown to the earth; and a third of the trees were burned up, and all green grass was burned up" (Rev. 8:7).

During a radio interview, Hal Lindsey commented on how he sought the opinion of military experts on the possibility of nuclear war being portrayed in the Bible. The experts had concluded that the re-entry of MIRV's (Multiple Independent Re-entry Vehicles) or multiple nuclear warheads into the earth's atmosphere would look much like meteorites, or as John described, "The stars of heaven fell to the earth" (Rev. 6:13). In Revelation 6:14, John viewed the sky as having "receded as a scroll." According to the experts, this could be descriptive of the immediate aftereffect of a nuclear explosion. Also, when a nuclear weapon is detonated over water, it would appear as John beheld, "And something like a great mountain burning with fire was thrown into the sea" (Rev. 8:8).

Many other verses describe possible nuclear holocaust. Read for yourself about the seven seals (Rev. 6:1-17 and 8:1-5), the seven trumpets (Rev. 8:9-21 and 11:15-19), and the seven bowls of wrath (Rev. 16:1-21).

God has permitted man to develop destructive nuclear capability. But God is not limited to man's inventions or activities when bringing His word to pass. "Then the fourth angel poured out his bowl on the sun . . . and men were scorched with great heat" (Rev. 16:8, 9). Jesus mentioned, "The sun will be darkened, and the moon will not give its light" (Matt. 24:29). This is exactly what would happen if the sun were to nova. Initially, it would become enlarged and intensely bright, then noticeably dim. Jesus predicted, "The stars will fall from heaven, and the powers of the heavens will be shaken" (Matt. 24:29b). Peter elaborated on this: "The heavens will pass away with a loud noise, and the elements will be dissolved with fire, and the earth and the works that are upon it will be burned up" (2 Pet. 3:10 RSV). Both have described what many scientists believe to be the future collapse of the universe. The power that causes the sun to nova, the earth to burn up, and the universe to move off its foundation and pass away, is far more potent than any nuclear warhead.

According to the Scriptures, the world will end due to God's direct intervention, not as a result of unlimited nuclear war. However, the probability of limited nuclear warfare producing much havoc upon the earth in the last days is almost a certainty because of the Bible's allusion to such activity. God has chosen to use man's ignorance—even his willful disobedience as well as his faithfulness—to establish His eternal purposes. Yes, God does have everything under control.

The question may not be *will* nuclear war occur, but *when!* Most believers feel it safe to presume nuclear war will not happen before the Rapture of the Church, and, using this premise, they conclude America will remain a free nation until then. Of course they use Scripture to prove their positions. The Bible is infallible, but interpretations are not. I don't claim to have the ultimate insight to the sequence of these eschatological events, but with these in mind, I will present a few of my own conclusions in the light of what I believe the Bible has to say.

If we were to have a nuclear confrontation before the Rapture of the Church, one would assume from what is portrayed in the Bible that the Great Tribulation would have already begun. This is why those who believe in the Pre-Tribulation view of the Rapture are convinced the Church will be taken out of the world before another nuclear war occurs. Since we've already had one nuclear conflict before the Rapture as well as before the Great Tribulation, it is conceivable another one could take place. However, with today's abundance of nuclear armament, the world is assured a greater amount of devastation than in the last nuclear conflict, unless one side has a distinct first-strike advantage as we did with Japan.

Israel and Russia

The book of Ezekiel depicts a full-scale conflict

with Russia and her allies arrayed against Israel. This major confrontation described by Ezekiel is the primary reason I believe it is scripturally possible for nuclear war to occur before the Rapture of the Church. "Surely in that day there shall be a great earthquake in the land of Israel . . . And I will bring Him [Gog] to judgment with pestilence and bloodshed; I will rain down on him, on his troops, and on the many peoples who are with him, flooding rain, great hailstones, fire, and brimstone" (Ezek. 38:19, 22).

This great battle will not be confined to just the mountains of Israel; it will have worldwide proportions. "I will send fire on Magog [Russia] and on those who live in security in the coastlands (other nations). Then they shall know that I am the Lord" (Ezek. 39:6).

In view of Israel's meticulous and time-consuming burial of the enemy dead following the war (see Ezek. 39:11-16), it is very possible that Ezekiel's vision included the aftermath of a nuclear holocaust as well.

This Russian-Israeli war is often interpreted to transpire after the Rapture of the Church at the conclusion of the Great Tribulation period, or during the Tribulation. However, I believe the Bible clearly states that the battle described in the book of Ezekiel is an entirely different conflict and will be fought before the other ones take place.

The book of Ezekiel lists a specific number of nations, led by Russia, that will attack Israel. "Thus saith the Lord God; Behold, I am against thee, O Gog, the chief prince of Meshech and Tubal: and I will turn thee back, and put hooks into thy jaws, and I will bring thee forth, and all thine army . . . Persia, Ethiopia, and Libya . . . Gomer, and all his bands; the house of

To-gärmah of the north quarters, and all his bands: and many people with thee" (Ezek. 38:3-6 KJV).

In *World War III and the Destiny of America,* Charles R. Taylor accurately identified these end-time assailants of the Holy Land.

> "Gog" is the "chief prince" of Magog (Russia) of the land controlled by Meshech and Tubal (Moscow and Tobolsk: the U.S.S.R).[6]

Most Bible scholars inform us that Magog refers to the present-day nation of Russia. The 1910 Scofield Reference Bible confirms Taylor's identification of Magog; it says "the primary reference is the northern (European) powers headed by Russia. ... The reference to Meshech and Tubal (Moscow and Tobolsk) is a clear mark of identification."[7] Both Unger's and Wycliffe's Bible commentaries concur that the descendants of Gog, an Israelite, traveled north of Asia Minor into Russia.

Taylor Defines Gog's Allies

> "Persia" is the ancient Persian Empire area from West Pakistan to Turkey to Egypt, except Saudia Arabia which was never conquered.
>
> "Ethiopia" is Ethiopia, Somalia, and Sudan of today.
>
> "Libya" is the Northern African Arab nation of today.
>
> "Gomer and his bands" is the Warsaw Pact area of Eastern Europe.
>
> "To-garmah of the north quarters" is the Baltic States area of Russia which

was Estonia, Lithuania, and Latvia.

To-garmah was a son of Gomer who was a grandson of Noah. Part of his family settled in Turkey, and part went to the Baltic region, thus referred to as being "of the north quarters."[8]

Prior to reaching Jerusalem, Gog will be killed along with his army (Ezek. 39:4-6). The Lord will send fire on Magog and on those who live in security in the coastlands. The nation of Israel will bury the enemy dead and burn their weapons for fuel (Ezek. 39:9-16).

Ezekiel 38:13 also mentions a group of neutral nations: "Sheba, Dedan, the merchants of Tarshish, and all their young lions," who will for whatever reason stand on the sidelines and say to Gog, "Have you come to take plunder? Have you gathered your army to take booty, to carry away silver and gold, to take away livestock and goods, to take great plunder?"

Tracing the descendants of "Sheba, Dedan, and the merchants of Tarshish, and all their young lions" is speculative at best. But *Unger's Bible Dictionary* renders a plausible identification.

> Sheba
> The kingdom of Sheba. The kingdom of the Sabeans (*q.v.*), which, according to some, embraced the greater part of the Yemen, or Arabia Felix.[9] Modern Yemen, or Arabia Felix, includes the southern part of Saudi Arabia, Yemen, People's Democratic Republic of Yemen, Oman, United Arab Emirates, and Qatar.

Dedan
> ... Jokshan, or a son of Jokshan, by intermarriage with the Cushite Dedan, formed a tribe of the same name, which appears to have had its chief settlement in the borders of Idumea.[10] Idumea or Edom was located in present-day Jordan.

Tarshish
> This is a Phoenician word from the Akkadian meaning smelting plant or refinery. ... Phoenician boats [the merchants of Tarshish] used to ply the sea regularly, transporting smelted ores from the mining towns in Sardinia and Spain.[11]

The ancient Phoenician Empire was centered in what is now Lebanon. According to Unger, the Phoenicians sailed north of Spain to secure tin from Cornwall, Britain.[12]

Many theologians conclude that Great Britain, whose navy once ruled the waves, is the latter-day "Merchants of Tarshish" described by Ezekiel, "all their young lions" being the United States of America, Canada, Australia, and New Zealand.

The War that will end the Great Tribulation Period and usher in the 1,000-year Millenium will begin with an attack upon Jerusalem and Judah by the beast or antichrist and all the kings of the earth. (Rev. 16:13, 14). The invasion will be temporarily successful. "The city [Jerusalem] shall be taken, the houses rifled, and the women ravished. Half of the city shall go into captivity, but the remnant of the people shall not be cut off from the city" (Zech. 14:2). In the midst of certain defeat, Jesus will suddenly return and bring victory to Israel. "Then the Lord will go forth and fight against those nations, as He fights in the day of battle. And in that day His feet will stand on the Mount of Olives which faces Jerusalem on the east" (vv. 14:3, 4). The war will conclude with what the Bible calls the Battle of Armageddon (Rev. 16:16). In this battle, the beast and the false prophet are captured alive and thrown into the lake of fire, and the armies that followed them are slain by the sword of the Lord (Rev. 19:20, 21). Immediately after the battle, Christ will rule and reign on this earth with His saints for 1,000 years (Rev. 20:4). Note: The theological term "Millennium" (meaning 1,000 in Latin) is used to describe this period.

Two Different Battles. When comparing the two battles, the dissimilarities are many. The prophet Ezekiel named a specific number of nations fighting against Israel (Ezek. 38:5, 6), whereas the combat at the end of the Great Tribulation pits "the kings of the earth and of the *whole world*" against Jerusalem (Rev. 16:14, emphasis added). In Zechariah 14:2, the Lord declares, "I will gather all the nations to battle against Jerusalem."

The book of Ezekiel mentions a number of nations who will remain neutral during the battle between Russia and Israel (Ezek. 38:13). The Scriptures do not allude to any neutral nations during the war at the end of the Great Tribulation.

In the struggle concluding the Great Tribulation, the enemy will conquer half of Jerusalem (Zech. 14:4). In Ezekiel's battle, the enemy will never reach Jerusalem. " 'You shall fall upon the mountains of Israel . . . You shall fall on the open field; for I have spoken,' says the Lord God" (Ezek. 39:4, 5).

Gog, the leader of Magog (Russia) will be killed along with the rest of his army in the battle in the book of Ezekiel (Ezek. 39:4, 11). The beast, the leader of the enemy in the war at the conclusion of the Great Tribulation, will be captured and "cast alive into the lake of fire burning with brimstone" (Rev. 19:20).

In Ezekiel's battle, the enemy dead are buried (Ezek. 39:11-16). But in the conflict that ends the Great Tribulation the enemy dead "shall not be lamented, or gathered, or buried; they shall become refuse on the ground" (Jer. 25:33).

Conclusion. There are just too many scriptural discrepancies between the military encounter described in the book of Ezekiel and the confrontation found in the Bible depicting the war at the end of the Great Tribulation for them to be the same battle.

When will Ezekiel's battle take place? After Israel defeats Russia, God will gather the birds of the air and the beasts of the field to feast upon the enemy slain for an unspecified amount of time (Ezek. 39:17-20). Israel will then, for seven months, bury whatever is left, after which a number of Israelites will be regularly employed for however long it takes to bury the last remaining enemy bone (vv. 13-16). Israel will also burn the enemy weapons for fuel for seven years. These events are significant as to when the battle in the book of Ezekiel will be fought. This type of activity would rule out this conflict occurring at the end of the Great Tribulation or during it. After the Great Tribulation, during the 1,000-year Millennial reign of Christ and His saints on earth, the planet will be a virtual paradise. There will be no need for the Jews to burn weapons for fuel or to bury bones to cleanse the land. During the last three and one-half years of the Great Tribulation period, it would be impossible for the Jews to systematically burn weapons or organize search parties to bury bones while the antichrist is relentlessly endeavoring to conquer Israel and exterminate the Jewish people. (Rev. 11:2; Zech. 14:2). During this time, two thirds of the Jews living in Israel will be killed (Zech. 13:8, 9). Many Jews will flee from Israel into the wilderness to a place prepared for them by God (Isa. 16:3-5; Rev. 12:6, 14).

The burning of the weapons and the burying of the bones will have to begin at least seven years prior to the final three and one-half years of the seven-year Great Tribulation Period. This calculation would place Ezekiel's battle at least three and one-half years before the beginning of the Great Tribulation Period, thus prior to the Rapture of the Church.

Current Events

Why have so many Christian theologians interpreted the Scriptures as saying the war in Ezekiel will take place after the Rapture? Maybe they subconsciously want to keep from thinking the impossible—nuclear war in our time—which would logically occur if Russia were to attack Israel before the Rapture of the Church.

Russia has recently rearmed Syria and has continued to supply the P.L.O. with military hardware. Lybia, Iraq and Ethiopia are already supportive of Russia's communist goals. Afghanistan is being pummelled. Iran lies in ruin under the Khomeini. And though the Moslem world has no love for Russia or communism, they have a greater hatred for Israel. The battle is shaping up.

Right now there are two things preventing the Soviet Union from marching against Israel: the sovereignty of God and the United States of America. Will Russia attack America with nuclear weapons before they assault Israel? Or will America stand passively by, powerless, afraid of Soviet retaliation? Either way the prognosis isn't good. I fear if we continue to try and scripturally evade this dilemma by means of eschatological escapism, the results will be far worse than anyone could ever imagine.

Russia's Nuclear Might. In view of biblical prophecy, the Soviet Union's relentless buildup of its nuclear arsenal over the past two decades, coupled with the gradual leveling off of America's nuclear strength, has greatly increased the likelihood of a Soviet pre-emptive nuclear first strike against, or nuclear blackmail of, the United States. Twenty years ago it would have been virtually impossible for the Soviets to launch a nuclear first strike against America. In 1965 the London-based International Institute for Strategic Studies (IIFSS) reported that America's long-range Intercontinental Ballistic Missile (ICBM) arsenal outnumbered the Russians' 854 to 270. Instead of striving to maintain nuclear superiority, our government failed to realize the communist goal of world conquest and embarked on a less expensive strategy of Mutual Assured Destruction (MAD). The purpose of this strategy is to retain only enough nuclear punch to retaliate and destroy the enemy after having suffered a nuclear first strike. (We hope that the enemy, knowing this, would refrain from attacking.)

Through the negotiation of the Strategic Arms Limitation Treaties, SALT I and SALT II, our government allowed Russia to play nuclear catch-up. By mid-1985, the Soviet Union had equalled or surpassed America in almost every category of nuclear hardware. The Soviets forged ahead in the crucial area of nuclear first-strike weaponry. Russia had deployed 1,398 ICBM's to America's 1,018. But even more threatening, the Soviet Union's ICBM land-based system had amassed a 6-to-2 warhead advantage, and was capable of delivering four times as much megatonnage* (firepower) as the American system.[13] The unabated Soviet effort to increase their nuclear first-strike advantage has motivated our government to continue to develop the controversial MX missile.

I haven't taken second-strike offensive weapons into consideration in my brief comparison of the United States' and Soviet Union's nuclear strength. Bombers are too slow and submarines too inaccurate to knock out the other nation's first-strike land-based weapons. These secondary delivery systems, though a deterrrent, are merely retaliatory by nature. But here too the Soviets have made great strides and are practically on an equal footing with the United States.

Star Wars. America's nuclear first-strike inferiority, coupled with the superior Soviet space weapons technology, has opened what is technically called the "window of vulnerability." On ABC's October 4, 1982, edition of *Nightline,* Dr. Robert Jastrow, space expert, brought to the American public's attention the killer satellites stationed in space by the Soviets. Dr. Jastrow reported how the Russians have tested these weapons twenty different times in the last ten years, successfully destroying ten test satellites. "They (the tests)

---

* One megaton is equal to 1,000,000 tons of TNT.

involve blowing up the killer satellites so that the shrapnel will disable the target satellite," explained Dr. Jastrow. When asked by *Nightline* anchorman Ted Koppel if he could substantiate his information, Dr. Jastor replied, "It is possible to track these orbits and to discover that these tests have occurred by radar."[14]

On February 28, 1983, along with many other Americans, I heard this item on the six o'clock news: "A United States reconnaisance satellite has been immobilized over the Soviet Union by a laser beam." No further comment on the incident was made on that broadcast. There was very little mention of it in any newspaper or magazine, either. In case you didn't know, the reconnaissance satellite is America's sole early-warning system against nuclear attack. Without it we are defenseless. In addition to detecting a nuclear first strike, satellites carry 75% of all military communications.

Was this bulletin of an immobilized reconnaissance satellite a hoax fabricated by our government to foster support for a space weapons buildup, or did our government censor the reporting of the actual event? It makes you wonder what's going on up there. Have the Russians done this sort of thing before? Have we knocked out any of their satellites? Who knows? I for one would like to know. The American people have a right to know the facts.

Russia, besides possessing killer satellites, has more advanced space weapons technology than does America, according to a U.S. Defense Department report, "Soviet Military Power 1985," which states, "The USSR's high-energy laser program . . . is much larger than the U.S. effort." The Soviets also "have begun to develop at least three types of high-energy laser weapons for air defense." In the report's initial briefing, Defense Secretary Casper W. Weinberger stated, "They [the Soviets] have progressed beyond technology research and they're actually developing prototype laser weapons. They've already got ground-based lasers that could be used to interfere with American and allied satellites. And they could have prototype space-based, anti-satellite laser weapons by the end of the decade."

"They could have prototypes for ground-based lasers for ballistic missile defense by the late 1980's. And they could begin testing of the components for large-scale development systems in the 1990's," Weinberger added.[15]

The Freeze. In light of communism's ultimate goal of world conquest, it would be unrealistic for our nation not to increase its nuclear first-strike capability or develop the "Star Wars" program as a deterrent against Soviet aggression. The hope that a nuclear freeze would display a nonprovoking stance towards the Soviet Union and thereby provide a reasonable safeguard against them is both naive and dangerous.

Andrei Sakhorov, well-known Russian physicist and architect of Russia's nuclear arsenal, expressed his fears in an open letter to his American friend and fellow physicist, Sidney Drell, of a potential Soviet nuclear first strike attack against the United States because of America's overall nuclear inferiority. Sakharov theorizes the Soviets would count on America "capitulating for the sake of saving what could be saved"[16] instead of striking back and committing all-out nuclear suicide. (Both sides have enough nuclear armament to waste each other and this planet many times over.)

If America is to attain nuclear parity with the Soviet Union and thereby deter a Soviet pre-emptive nuclear first strike, then "that price must be paid," said Sakharov, by the continuation of the arms race by the U.S. until the Soviets are ready to disarm.

Sakharov, who is not a Christian, reinforced in his letter his belief in America's need to continue the arms race, reminding us that "since 1945 there has been a relentless expansion of the Soviet sphere of influence [that] has today assumed proportions dangerously harmful to international equilibrium."

I pray that America's leaders would heed the words of this man "crying in the wilderness" (Matt. 3:3). Mr. Sakharov probably knows more of the Kremlin's ways and the intricacies of its military network than do all our analysts combined.

Although military preparedness is essential to the freedom of any nation, all the missiles in the world will not protect a nation that God has consigned to judgment because of its disobedience. "Righteousness [not armament] exalts a nation, but sin is a reproach to any people" (Prov. 14:34).

Summary. The three major reasons nuclear war is possible before the Rapture are: 1) the Bible's prophetic picture of end-time events, especially the battle between Russia and Israel as foretold in the book of Ezekiel, 2) current world conditions, including the aligning of the Arab nations with the Soviet Union, and 3) Russia's superior nuclear first-strike capability.

Footnotes to Part 3

1. Merril F. Unger, *Unger's Bible Dictionary*, 3rd. ed. (Chicago: Moody Press, 1966), p. 796.
2. Glanville Downey, *Antioch In the Age of Theodosius the Great*, The Centers of Civilization Series, 6th Series (Norman, OK: Oklahoma University Press, 1962), p. 25.
3. Richard Pipes, *Russia Under the Old Regime* (New York: Charles Scribner's Sons, 1974), p. 242.
4. *The Random House Dictionary of the English Language* (New York: Simon and Schuster, 1966), p. 706.
5. David Wilkerson, *The Vision* (Old Tappan, NJ: Fleming H. Revell Company, 1974), p. 116.
6. Charles R. Taylor, *World War III and the Destiny of America* (Nashville: Thomas Nelson Publishers, 1979), p. 161-2.
7. *The Scofield Reference Bible*, ed. C.I. Schofield, D.D. (New York: Oxford University Press, 1945), p. 883.
8. Taylor, *World War III.* p. 162.
9. Unger, *Bible Dictionary.* p. 1006.
10. Ibid., p. 258.
11. Ibid., p. 1070-1.
12. Ibid., p. 862.
13. Stockholm International Peace Research Institute (SIPRI), *Military Balance*, 1985, pp. 180-1.
14. © American Broadcasting Companies, Inc., 1982.
15. Reported in the Plainfield, NJ, *Courier News*, April 3, 1985.
16. Excerpts of Andrei Sakharov's letter, written while under house arrest, appeared in *Time Magazine* July 4, 1983.

PART 4
America's Judgment

We've studied the principles God has set forth in Scripture for dealing with disobedient nations and individuals, and we've reviewed America's current condition in light of those principles, as well as history's record. Therefore, it shouldn't come as any surprise to you to hear that the United States of America has been under God's judgment for the past twenty-five years, with worse judgments yet to come. And unless there is a great repentance throughout the land we can expect God to visit us with these specific judgments: limited nuclear war, followed by an invasion of communist troops, with Americans being carried away as slaves to foreign lands.

These words of judgment are not penned with malice. I love America. I desire God's best for this land, and so does God. I pray that these words will not be misunderstood or discounted or for whatever reason rejected, but will inspire revival in the heart of every Christian in America, and bring salvation to every non-Christian. This was God's reasoning when instructing Jeremiah to write down all the words that He had spoken to him against Israel, Judah, and all the nations. "It may be," wished God, "that the house of Judah will hear all the adversities which I purpose to bring upon them, that everyone may turn from his evil way, that I may forgive their iniquity and their sin" (Jer. 36:3).

When God warns of judgment it isn't only done with the intent of sending judgment, but also to foster conviction of sin. God longs for repentance.

This enables God to show mercy to those who deserve otherwise, thereby restoring them to a right relationship with himself.

Israel's Example. "The Lord is merciful and gracious, slow to anger, and abounding in mercy" (Ps. 103:8). Therefore when God does send judgment, it is usually a gradual process, slowly increasing in severity over an extended period of time. A good illustration of this is found in the book of Amos, where the Lord, speaking through the prophet Amos, reviewed the different judgments that had already befallen Israel's ten northern tribes. " 'Also I gave you cleanness of teeth [famine] in all your cities. And lack of bread in all your places; yet you have not returned to Me,' says the Lord. 'I also withheld rain from you, when there were still three months to the harvest. I made it rain on one city, I withheld rain from another city. One part was rained upon, and where it did not rain the part withered. . . . I blasted you with blight and mildew. When your gardens increased, your vineyards, your fig trees, and your olive trees, the locust devoured them; yet you have not returned to Me,' says the Lord. 'I sent among you a plague after the manner of Egypt; your young men I killed with a sword . . . I overthrew some of you, as God overthrew Sodom and Gommorrah, and you were like a firebrand plucked from the burning; yet you have not returned to Me,' says the Lord" (Amos 4:6, 7, 9, 11).

The Lord, having sent these various calamities, then informed stubborn Israel, "Prepare to meet your God" (Amos 4:12). The Lord, still hoping Israel would return to Him, mercifully withheld the final and most severe judgment, the conquering Assyrian army, another fifty-six years.

11
Under Judgment

Although this book will not present the total picture of God's dealing with America, and by no means is it the final word, the prophecies, visions, dreams and revelations I am going to share with you are a small yet balanced portion of what God has been saying to America through the Body of Christ. I will, with God's help, do my best to give you these prophetic exposes exactly as they were given to me by those who received them.

We ought to give heed to what God says to America through His prophetic Word since there is a total lack of specific references to America in the written Word. Some scholars have speculated that America is one of the "young lions" of Tarshish [England] (Ezek. 38:13), or the land "beyond the rivers of Ethiopia" (Isa. 18:1), or one of those "who live in security in the coastlands" (Ezek. 39:6). According to their interpretation of Scripture, the Pilgrims concluded that this newly settled land was the nation of Israel restored. On the other hand, the non-appearance of America in the

Scriptures is considered confirmation by Hal Lindsey, and other authorities on the book of Revelation, of America's continual decline, and of its eventual absence as a viable force in our Father's business and in world affairs during the end times. On the other hand, the Scriptures' failure to mention America (along with most of the world) has led some to believe that America could experience great revival before our Lord's return.

No certain conclusion can be drawn from the above theories: thus the immense importance of the prophetic Word. However, the prophetic Word must conform with the principles and directives found in Scripture that apply to all nations in order to be valid.

Note: The prophetic Word, though relevant to America's present situation, is by no means an addition to, or a substitute for, God's written Word, "the Holy Scriptures, which are able to make you wise for salvation through faith which is in Christ Jesus" (2 Tim. 3:15).

I have limited the judgment and revival prophecies in this book, for the most part, to those either mentioning the United States of America by name or containing specific information about America; to do otherwise would require an encyclopedic volume.

I pray that you will not harden your heart at the ensuing words in this book. They won't be very pleasant or appealing, but I believe them to be true. All I ask is for you to read them, then judge for yourself.

Dear friends, "do not believe every spirit, but test the spirits" (1 John 4:1) to see whether they are from God; weigh carefully what I have said.

Before depicting America's coming judgments, it is first necessary to briefly review some prophecies that state God has already visited America with judgment.

"Wrath Upon the Land"

On January 27, 1961, in Sarasota, Florida, Robert Lambert and two other brethren beheld an unusual vision pertaining to God's judgment of America. The following account was written by Gerald Derstine, president of Gospel Crusade, Inc., in Bradenton, Florida, and appeared in the April 1, 1961, issue of *Harvest Time* magazine.

"At five o'clock [in the morning] I heard a knocking on my door, with someone crying out, 'Brother Derstine! Brother Derstine!' When I opened the door, one of the men, trembling all over, pleaded: 'Oh, Brother Derstine, please lay your hands upon me and pray for me! God gave me a vision of the wrath of God, the judgment God is going to send upon the world and upon our land. Oh, my God, my God, I wish I had not seen this. . . .'

"Upon returning to the room where he and the two other men had been sleeping, the Lord came into a portion of the room and the power and the brightness was so intense that the men shielded their eyes with their arms and cried out for the Lord not to come any closer, for they could not stand His presence! The fear of God was upon them. Then the Lord spoke through Brother Robert Lambert, as his voice and his whole being took on a different form, giving forth this message: 'Write this down; this is of the Lord! THE VILENESS AND THE WICKEDNESS OF MAN HAVE COME UP BEFORE ME AS A STINK IN MY NOSTRILS AND I WILL NOT BE ABLE TO STAY

MY HAND ANY LONGER. I AM SICK TO MY STOMACH. THE MOCKERY OF MY WORD IN THE RELIGIOUS SYSTEMS OF AMERICA ARE AN ABOMINATION TO ME. I HAVE COME TO MY BURSTING POINT AND WILL SPEW OUT MY WRATH UPON THE LAND. . . .' "

The next morning a group of believers assembled in Gerald Derstine's office ". . . to hear in more detail what happened through the night concerning the vision by Bro. Lambert. For four hours he admonished us and prophesied to us under a strong anointing of the Holy Spirit. Sometimes he would tremble and shake; sometimes he would kneel. It was as though God was speaking directly to us! It was awesome! The Lord declared: 'The wrath of God, the Day of the Lord, is here now! These things shall be known around the earth! There will be others, this particular morning, that will know that this is the hour, and that I am not going to wait any longer!' "

God always confirms His Word. Three other brethren had the same exact type of vision on the same night as brother Lambert did. "The next evening, we had a service for the public and a minister from Orlando, Florida was led of the Spirit to come to this particular meeting to have fellowship with us. He did not know about the visitation we had, until he heard the speaker relating the testimony of the great vision. With great fear, this visiting minister of Orlando told us of his terrible dream (vision) he had the same night concerning the great wrath of God coming upon our land. He told us he saw such terrible things that he wished he would have never seen this dream. This was identical to the vision Bro. Lambert had on the same night. Three days later we received a letter from missionaries from Haiti telling us of a great unusual visitation of God which they experienced on the night of January 27. The missionary, in writing this letter, stated what his wife experienced in her vision that particular night: 'The Lord showed her terrible persecutions that are coming on the earth and how that men will be killed and maimed. She saw a large city whose buildings were falling upon people and huge fires were to be seen everywhere....' "

Several days later brother Derstine spoke at the Regional Convention of the Full Gospel Business Men's Fellowship International in Washington, D.C. In his message, brother Derstine proclaimed what the Lord had revealed to the brethren in Florida. Then "...a man from Kitchener, Ontario, Canada who stood to his feet and trembling, began to tell the congregation in this meeting that he also had an identical vision from the Lord of the great wrath of God coming on the North American continent. He said it was such a terrible sight, he wished he had not experienced this. The significant fact was that his vision also came on the same night as the other three afore-mentioned."

As time passed, J. Preston Ebby, a former associate pastor of the Revival Tabernacle in Sarasota, Florida, and one of the men who was with brother Lambert the morning he shared his vision, wondered whether or not he and the others had misunderstood what God had revealed to them. He expressed his feelings in an article entitled "America Under Judgment," which appeared in the February 1981 issue of *End Times Digest*. "Over and over again we received the message: The Day of the Lord is—NOW! The judgment of America is—NOW! 'I shall pour out My wrath upon this people and upon this land—NOW!' So terrible were these words that I literally walked about for days gazing into the sky, fully expecting to see Russian missiles attacking any mintue . . .!"

"Years later as I meditated upon the visitation I asked, 'Lord, did we misunderstand you? Where is the judgment you promised?' Then suddenly, like a bolt of lightning flashing from within some tortuous cloud, the revelation burst upon my astonished spirit as a vast panorama of events spread clear as crystal before my wondering eyes. I saw! I understood! The judgment *has come* exactly as prophesied! The judgment *is here!* NOW! And like a gigantic tidal wave rushing through the sea it surges on to a swift and certain conclusion!

"In my opinion there is no greater certainty than that the judgments of God upon our beloved country began just when God declared they did—in 1961! It should be clear to any man or woman with one eye to see and half sense, that during the past two decades America's *power, pride, prestige,* and *purpose* HAVE BEEN BROKEN!"

Brother Ebby concluded his article with a rather lengthy dissertation on how America's myriad failures over the past two decades can be attributed to this nation being under God's judgment. These failures include the Bay of Pigs invasion, the Russian missile crisis, the U-2 incident, President Kennedy's assassination, the hippie movement, the Viet Nam War, Watergate, the Iranian hostage crisis, and worldwide communist expansion.

I totally agree with brother Ebby and with the other men and women of God: the United States of America is under God's judgment.

God vividly revealed this truth to me after a severe winter northeaster pummeled the Atlantic coast. The next morning, as I was driving by Washington Rock State Park in New Jersey, I saw an American flag in shreds, but still flying. After I had driven by it, the Lord said to me, 'This nation is torn.' I began to weep, knowing the torn flag was symbolic of America's already being under the judgment of God.

12
Future Judgments

Since our nation's beginning, God's servants, George Washington among them, have caught glimpses of what we could expect if we did not heed God's warnings. Within the last few decades, through more detailed prophecies, God has been disclosing that He is about to increase the severity of the judgments He is sending upon us.

A Map and a Shroud

In a vision, Kay Fowler* witnessed the end of America's freedom.

---

* Over the past several years Kay Fowler has received numerous visions and dreams concerning God's judgment of America. Sister Fowler, a housewife, mother, and member of an interdenominational church, resides in Horse Shoe, North Carolina. She says, "As the revelations continued a message began to unfold." Kay has recorded her prophetic story on tape. Any prophecy in this book ascribed to Kay Fowler has been copied from her tape with permission. If you wish to learn more about her message for America, write:
Kay Fowler
Box 221-C, Horse Shoe, NC 28742

"I saw a map of the United States and it was covered with blood. And the blood started to flow from the right side of the map until the entire map was covered. At another time I saw people in an auditorium, and they were singing and shedding tears because of their love for America. And they were singing "America the Beautiful." After the singing stopped, I received the word "Shroud—shroud to cover America." Of course a shroud is a burial cloth. I believe America as a nation is going to dwindle; she's going to die. And the freedoms that we know today will cease to be."

"The Lord Shall Bring a Nation Against Thee"

Through this vision Kay Fowler saw judgment coming to America by means of a foreign nation.

"In November of 1980 I had a vision of part of the Scripture in the book of Deuteronomy, Chapter 28:49, 50. It was early one morning and I was awakened; and there before me on the wall and in full color was the unveiling of this Scripture—'The Lord shall bring a nation against thee from afar, from the end of the earth, as swift as the eagle flieth; a nation whose tongue thou shalt not understand; a nation of fierce countenance, of which shall not regard the person of the old, nor show favor to the young.' "

Two Storms

In another vision Kay Fowler saw judgment portrayed as storms, symbolizing war.

"The form of judgment that will be on this nation that I've seen will be in the form of war. One of the first revelations God gave me concerning this judgment was a map of the United States of America. As I saw it before me, there stood a weatherman to the right, and as he was speaking he said, 'There's a giant storm headed towards America, it is coming from the Soviet Union.' As I looked out to the left in the waters, I saw a great black storm cloud headed for the states. The voice continued to speak, 'There's a smaller storm that will precede, and it will hasten the coming and will draw in right behind it the larger storm. As I looked I could see the smaller storm cloud drift over the country and stop. Now at this present time I have no knowledge what this smaller storm represents. At one time I thought it could be the Iranian crisis. And certainly it could possibly be the economic peril that is facing our country."

The smaller storm that is already here represents judgments of lesser magnitude compared to the larger storm, which is yet to come.

Destroyed by Fire

I stayed with brother Frank Matthews and his family during the "Washington for Jesus" rally in April 1980. While there, he told me of a vision he had seen earlier that same year of Washington, D.C.

> The wickedness of Washington, D.C., was so great that the Lord told me He was going to judge the city and the people in it. He told me to warn to brethren to escape the judgment that was to come. Some heeded, but most did not. A number of the saints began to intercede for the city, and judgment was postponed for a season. Then once again the Lord prompted me to warn the brethren of the coming judgment, and as

before only a few heeded the warning. The day came when the Lord told me to leave the city. Shortly thereafter God's judgment fell upon Washington. And from up in the surrounding hills, as far as my eye could see I saw large areas of the city had burned with fire, while smaller sections interspersed among them were hardly touched. Here and there I would notice a house that wasn't damaged by the fire, while the houses on either side of it were destroyed. The homes and areas that escaped destruction were those where much intercession was made. I clearly saw people praying and moving around in the city. I and the other saints who obeyed God were saved, and provision was made for us.

At the time of this writing the Lord has not yet directed brother Matthews to leave Washington, D.C. However, He has led him to share this vision with the believers in the greater Washington area, and exhort them to intercede for our nation's capitol but not to partake of its wickedness.

Hurricane of Fire

In this vision Kay Fowler beheld God's judgment as a great fire consuming our nation.

"At one time I saw a hurricane of fire. I had been placed out in the middle of this great field to be a watchman for my family and some members of my congregation. They were standing in a building behind me, waiting for my signal. I was out standing in a field alone watching this great hurricane of fire approaching, covering many, many miles at a time. It looked just like a hurricane that I've seen in pictures, but instead of walls of water it was walls of fire. The fire was burning and catching everything that it was touching on fire. The fire was burning in the trees, the woods, and on the mountainside.

"I was giving hand signals back to my family—signals such as one might see a flight attendant standing on a runway signaling for airplanes to land. As the storm moved closer, I continued with the signals, and then saw that the fire was burning in the middle of our trees, and getting very close to our building. So I ran to them and said, 'It's time to leave, the fire is here.' I led them out of the building for a distance to a little shelter. Inside of this place was blankets for warmth and maybe other supplies, but blankets were the only things I saw. As the last one moved into the shelter, the thought came to me to pray for rain to put out the fire. So I prayed in the name of Jesus that He would let it rain. Then I saw sprinkles of rain begin to fall all around, and I could hear sizzling of fire as the flames began to diminish. Then I saw the heavens open up and there before me stood a great lion. His eyes were as rubies and as coals of fire; at His feet lay a great sword. I knew Him to be the Lion of the Tribe of Judah. And I cried out loud: 'Yes, Lord—you are the King of kings and Lord of lords. You are the great Lion of the tribe of Judah.' I saw the sword at His feet; I knew it represented judgment, and that it was He that was in the hurricane of fire that was sent to bring judgment on America."

A Huge White Cloud

Robert T. Heath, a family man and local contractor from Scotch Plains, New Jersey, has also witnessed a vision of cataclysmic judgment coming upon America.

"Within the past couple of years, I have had a dream, the significance of which I am uncertain, but which gave me a confidence in the Lord's faithfulness towards believers who remain present when God's judgment comes to destroy the ungodly.

"I was facing New York City from New Jersey when I saw a huge white cloud hanging close to the ground and dispersing rapidly in all surrounding directions. I sensed immediate impending destruction of my physical being as I stood in a kind of braced position on open ground. I knew that within the intense heat of that coming cloud, that for me, there was safety. It was as if I knew that Jesus was in it for me, even though it would otherwise be an instrument of destruction for the world of unbelievers."

Author's note: Some of the prophecies in this section could very well describe a nuclear holocaust. They are also similar in scope to biblical prophecies depicting end-time events.

The Statue of Liberty

This extraordinary vision of future judgment was seen in 1954 by an anonymous American evangelist as he gazed through a telescope from the top of the Empire State Building in New York City. The Statue of Liberty vision in its entirety can be found in a book entitled *World War III and the Destiny of America* by Charles R. Taylor.[1]

"That which I was looking upon was not Manhattan Island. It was all of the North American continent spread out before me as a map is spread upon a table. It was not the East River and the Hudson River that I saw on either side, but the Atlantic and the Pacific Oceans. And instead of the Statue of Liberty standing there in the bay on her tiny island, I saw her standing far out in the Gulf of Mexico. She was between me and the United States.

"There, clear and distinct, lay all the North American continent, with all its great cities. To the north lay the Great Lakes. Far to the northeast was New York City. I could see Seattle and Portland far to the northwest. Down the West Coast, there was San Francisco and Los Angeles. Closer in the foreground, there lay New Orleans, at the center of the Gulf Coast area. I could see the great towering ranges of the Rocky Mountains, and trace with my eye the Continental Divide. All this and more I could see spread out before me as a great map upon a table.

"As I looked, suddenly from the sky I saw a giant hand reach down. That gigantic hand was reaching out toward the Statue of Liberty. In a moment her gleaming torch was torn from her hand, and in it instead was placed a cup. And I saw protruding from that cup a giant sword, shining, as if a great light had been turned upon its glistening edge. Never before had I seen such a sharp, glistening, dangerous sword. It seemed to threaten all the world. As the great cup was placed in the hand of the Statue of Liberty, I heard these words: 'Thus saith the Lord of hosts . . . Drink ye and be drunken, spue, and fall, and rise no more, because of the sword which I will send. . . .'

"As I heard these words, I recognized them as a quotation from Jeremiah 25:27. I was amazed to hear the Statue of Liberty speak out in reply, 'I will not drink'!

"Then, as the voice of thunder, I heard again the

voice of the Lord, saying: . . . 'Thus saith the Lord of hosts, Ye shall certainly drink' [Jer. 25:28].

"Then suddenly the giant hand forced the cup to the lips of the Statue of Liberty, and she became powerless to defend herself. The mighty hand of God forced her to drink every drop of the cup. As she drank the bitter dregs, these were the words that I heard: '. . . should ye be utterly unpunished? Ye shall not be unpunished: for I will call for a sword upon all the inhabitants of the earth, saith the Lord of hosts' [Jer. 25:29].

"When the cup was withdrawn from the lips of the Statue of Liberty, I noticed the sword was missing from the cup, which could mean but one thing. The contents of the cup had been completely consumed! I knew that the sword merely typified war, death, and destruction, which is no doubt on the way.

"Then, as one drunken on too much wine, I saw the Statue of Liberty become unsteady on her feet and begin to stagger and to lose her balance. I saw her splashing in the Gulf, trying to regain her balance. I saw her stagger again and again, and fall to her knees. As I saw her desperate attempts to regain her balance, and rise to her feet again, my heart was filled with compassion for her struggles. But as she struggled there in the Gulf, once again I heard these words: 'Ye shall drink and be drunken, and spue, and fall, and rise no more because of the sword that I shall send among you.' "

The next sequence of the "Statue of Liberty" vision depicted a skeleton-shaped black cloud spewing out white vapors upon America. The harmless-looking vapors reached the Statue of Liberty in the Gulf, causing her to cough violently.

"As I watched, the coughing grew worse. . . . The

Statue of Liberty was moaning and groaning. She was in mortal agony. The pain must have been terrific, as again and again she tried to clear her lungs of those horrible vapors. I watched her there in the Gulf as she staggered, clutching her lungs and her breasts with her hands. Then she fell to her knees. In a moment she gave one final cough, made a last desperate effort to rise to her knees, and then fell face-forward into the waters of the Gulf and lay still—still as death. Only the lapping of the waves, splashing over her body, which was partly under the water and partly out of the water, broke the stillness."

Author's note: While our nation is so concerned about restoring the statue, what she represents continues to deteriorate.

Nuclear War

There are a number of prophecies that refer directly to nuclear war taking place in America; by being aware of the scripturally based probability of its occurrence, we will be ready to consider, as unbearable and unrealistic as it may seem, the somber possibility of such a tragic event. If nuclear war comes to America, by mistake or by well-calculated plan, it will nevertheless be a judgment sent by God.

In his latest book, *Set the Trumpet to Thy Mouth*,[3] David Wilkerson proclaims that Russian nuclear warheads will suddenly and totally destroy America, and few will escape, and that our nation will suffer a nuclear holocaust because our cup of iniquity is full.

Huge Ball of Fire

A segment of the "Statue of Liberty" vision depicts a nuclear strike by submarines off America's coast.

The nuclear attack immediately followed the death of the Statue of Liberty in sequence, and no doubt produced the deadly vapors which caused Liberty's demise.

"Then suddenly I saw from the Atlantic and from the Pacific, and out of the Gulf, rocket-like objects that seemed to come up like fish leaping out of the water. High into the air they leaped, each heading into a different direction, but every one toward the United States. On the ground, the sirens screamed louder. Up from the ground I saw similar rockets beginning to ascend. To me, these appeared to be interceptor rockets, although they arose from different points all over the United States. However, none of them seemed to be successful in intercepting the rockets that had risen from the ocean on every side. These rockets finally reached their maximum height, slowly turned over, and fell back to earth in defeat. Then suddenly the rockets which had leaped out of the oceans like fish all exploded at once. The explosion was ear-splitting. The next thing which I saw was a huge ball of fire. The only thing I have ever seen which resembled that which I saw in my vision was the picture of the explosion of the H-bomb somewhere in the Pacific some months ago. In my vision, it was so real I seemed to feel a searing heat from it.

"As the vision spread before my eyes, and I viewed the widespread desolation brought about by the terrific explosions, I could not help thinking, 'While the defenders of our nation have quibbled over what measures of defense to use, and neglected the only true defense—faith and dependence upon the true and living God—that which she has greatly feared has come upon her! How true it has been proven that 'except the Lord keep the city, the watchman waketh but in vain.' "

In 1954, the time of this vision, submarines armed with nuclear missiles were unheard of.

Thermonuclear Warheads

In 1971 I saw, in a dream, limited nuclear war in America.

I beheld two or three short successive orange-colored flashes of light off in the distance towards the north. These flashes, which produced a strobe-light effect, literally lit up the nighttime sky. As they occurred I could briefly see the outline of some mountains from beyond which the flashes came. The next morning—in the dream—as I was walking through a field of swamp grass, I heard a news report over a transistor radio which was attached to a corner pole of a lean-to. The news report said: "Washington, D.C., New York City, Chicago, Denver and San Francisco have been struck by thermonuclear warheads." By the time the broadcast said "Denver" I was in the Spirit. I was standing beside Jesus. I then realized it was Jesus who was giving the news report, and what I was hearing over the transistor radio was the Word of God. As He spoke, His words could be heard throughout eternity. As Jesus said, "Denver," He pointed there, and as he did the Holy Spirit showed me, though it was not quite dawn, exactly where Denver was. It was still night in San Francisco, yet the Holy Spirit showed me where that city was too. I then looked back toward the East Coast. The sun had already risen there and, through some cirrocumulus clouds, I could see the Florida area. I suddenly realized I was up in the heavens looking down. I also knew that during this limited nuclear attack I would be in Florida very close to the Alabama border. Several years later I discovered that this part of Florida is indeed swampland, just as in the dream.

New York City After Nuclear War

Clinton White, author, evangelist, and former host of the radio program, "Let's Talk About Jesus," spoke over the airwaves one Saturday morning describing New York City after nuclear war. He stated that in his vision many buildings were destroyed; others were only half standing. There was much rubble strewn about the streets. The city was without electricity and other essential services. If that wasn't bad enough, brother White really shocked me when he mentioned there were still people living there. He could see them going about in the daytime, though there weren't nearly as many as there are now. He also saw those who ventured out after dark being attacked by packs of wild dogs that roamed the streets.

A Device

Brother White also told his radio audience that he saw in a dream a device bearing a hammer-and-sickle insignia make a soft landing on Mars. And as the device landed, he looked back towards the earth and saw small fires break out over every part of the globe. He understood the fires to be warfare. The first thing Clinton did when he awoke early the next morning was to turn on the radio, and immediately he heard these words: "The Russians have soft-landed a device on Mars." This was in 1974.

Nuclear Radiation

The night before I left Worcester, Massachusetts, to preach the Gospel in Florida, an anonymous Christian brother informed me of a startling dream he had experienced a few years earlier. In this dream, because he'd been preaching the Gospel, he was hidden away in a small cabin located in a wooded area by a lake. He thought it to be somewhere in New Hampshire. He mentioned how the natural surroundings, the trees, the grass, the lake, all seemed so beautiful, but he knew the lake was contaminated and unfit to drink. He had been provided with a canteen of water and a little food by the Christians who had brought him to this place of refuge. He had been there a few days when some travelers came passing through the area. He felt it safe to go out and speak with them. As he greeted the travelers, he realized there was something different about them—their skin was greyish white and blotchy, and their hair had fallen out in patches. However, they were not the least bit upset by their condition. He offered them some water from his canteen, but they refused, saying it didn't matter if they drank the water from the lake.

The travelers said it would take two to three years for the land and water to cleanse themselves. They also greatly encouraged the brother in hiding by ministering the things of the Lord to him. Before they left, they held hands and prayed for one another and embraced. The travelers then resumed their journey.

Some time after the dream, the brother went to a library and read descriptions of people who had been exposed to nuclear radiation; he immediately recognized their features—they were like those of the people in the dream.

Foreign Invasion

There certainly isn't anything more detrimental to any society than a foreign invasion, that is, unless it is preceded by a nuclear attack. These two judgments combined would be unparalleled in earth's history, and would cause America to far surpass all other nations in the amount of misery and woe experienced. Of course, if God were to send these two particular judgments upon America, the rest of the world would unquestionably suffer as well, but not as much as we would.

Troops Appeared

In this vision Kay Fowler watched as foreign troops placed a large segment of America's population in concentration camps or on ships.

"I saw troops had suddenly appeared on the land. And I found myself hidden away on top of a mountain. And I'm looking down through a periscope—I see the troops have appeared and have gathered together a great multitude of Americans. And they have surrounded them and I see fear on their faces. Suddenly, the troops divide the people into two great numbers. The loved ones are being divided—husbands and wives separated, and there's much shedding of tears.

"I saw a group on the right, and they were gathered to go up a ramp, possibly into a ship. I know it was a loading ramp or a gangplank. . . . Behind the second group, I could see small buildings, like barracks."

Russian Soldier

The anonymous Christian brother from Worcester, Massachusetts, also shared with me a dream he had of walking down a street in the United States with one arm around a Russian Soldier; in his other hand was a New Testament in the Russian language from which he was reading to the soldier. The brother read to the Russian soldier from the Gospel of John and also from the book of Romans.

Enemy Planes

In another vision, Kay Fowler witnessed the defeat of America's conventional forces by enemy invaders.

"I've also seen a large city with skyscrapers, and enemy planes were coming in and shelling the city. The buildings were on fire and burning as if bombs had been dropped. I saw the people all in a panic, fleeing the city for safety. I've seen New York City harbor completely destroyed. I watched as every ship rolled over and sank. I've seen military jets trying to land and take off from airstrips and then crash because untrained and unqualified people were placed in command positions. I've seen a squadron of our American jets flying to the war zone, excited about being in war. On each plane was an American flag. I could hear the pilots talking from the cockpit of each of these planes, boasting how powerful their planes were and how great America is. Then, I saw them crashing into the sides of the mountain. 'Though thou exalt thyself as the eagle, and though thou set thy nest among the stars, thence will I bring thee down, saith the Lord' (Obad. 1:4 KJV). In the same revelation I saw that when all the men are called off to the war zone all the work is left to the women in that community."

Full Battle Array

A Christian brother from Seattle, Washington, whom I met while telling of these coming judgments, related to me what he had seen in a vision concerning the western United States. Instead of combines and tractors, he beheld a large contingent of foreign troops in full battle array rolling through the wheat fields of what seemed to be eastern Washington State. The well-equipped army, which included planes, tanks, and armored vehicles, was rushing toward the battlefield. He knew they were foreign troops because their helmets and uniforms were not at all like ours, but distinctly European.

I Have Raised Up the Communists

Several years ago I read two of Dave Wilkerson's books, *The Vision* and *Racing Towards Judgment.* I became very troubled by them. I cried out to the Lord, "Is this man telling the truth? I've got to know." The Lord instructed me to read the book of Habakkuk. In the first chapter, Habakkuk prophesied the horrible Chaldean (Babylonian) invasion of Jerusalem. As I read the Scriptures, the Holy Spirit spoke to me, saying, "I have raised up the communists to bring judgment upon America." I began to tremble. It was as if I were there and the invasion had already happened. My spirit fainted within me and I had no hope left. After I had somewhat recovered, the Lord began to impress upon me through Habakkuk's prophecy certain aspects of a communist invasion of America.

"For indeed I am raising up the Chaldeans [representing the communists], a bitter and hasty nation which marches through the breadth of the earth, to possess dwelling places that are not theirs" (Hab. 1:6).

Communism can only survive by conquest—it must take in order to have.

"They are terrible and dreadful; their judgment and their dignity proceed from themselves" (v. 7). The communists have substituted fear and trepidation in place of justice.

"They all come for violence" (v. 9). Communism's belief that human beings are mere material objects has led to the highest number and grossest forms of violent acts on the battlefield and in prison camp known to man. In places such as Cambodia, Zimbabwe and Afghanistan, communism has proven to be a relentless butcher.

"They gather captives like sand" (v. 9b). Communism is a Satanic plot to enslave mankind.

"They scoff at kings, and princes are scorned by them" (v. 10). The communists haven't any respect for authority other than their own.

"They deride every stronghold, for they heap up mounds of earth and seize it" (v. 10b). Communism's doctrinal premise of eventual world conquest has inundated its followers with an insatiable appetite for revolution and war.

"Then they sweep by like the wind guilty men, whose own might is their god" (v. 11 RSV). The arm of flesh is the god of communism. As God sent the Chaldeans to execute judgment upon Jerusalem, He is sending the communists to judge America.

Carried Away to Foreign Lands

It has been the practice of conquerors down through the centuries to carry the spoils of war back to their own countries. The most valuable resource any nation has is its people. This is why 200,000 Jews, including

Daniel, Hananiah, Mishael and Azariah, were taken from their homes in Israel and Judah and brought to Assyria and Babylon. The next set of prophecies will primarily focus on Americans being carried away to foreign lands.

A number of prophecies in this book contain more than just one aspect of God's judgment on America. And perhaps no prophecy better portrays the total overall picture of judgment than the following.

And God Sent Prophets[3]

"God caused me to see what would happen if we continued to proscrastinate" ... the words of a prominent American evangelist who gives us the following story as God gave it to him.

"Between midnight and dawn the communists attacked America. Major cities were destroyed in a matter of minutes by long range missiles fired from Russia, and medium range missiles fired from submarines, stationed along our coasts.

"All communications were destroyed. This was synchronized with a widespread reign of terror, caused by communist saboteurs blowing up bridges, power plants, dams, etc. People fled to the mountains, deserts, and open fields, and there hunger, disease and death overtook them.

"In a couple of days thousands of Russian and Chinese soldiers were flown in to restore order. All leaders in the American way of life were immediately shot. A proclamation was issued by the communists for everyone to return to their homes, and they would be cared for and protected. Everyone was required to register with the communists, and at that time receive instructions to turn their property over to the state, with all money. All children were separated from their parents and made wards of the state.

"While this was happening all the remaining nations in the world surrendered to the local communists.

"The final blow came when ALL ADULT AMERICANS WERE SHIPPED OUT AS SLAVES TO EVERY NATION IN THE WORLD. Every nation was calling for American slaves so they could humiliate and utterly destroy the last vestige of Americanism.

"People from China, India and other overpopulated areas were brought to America to take the place of enslaved Americans that were being shipped out to every nation under the sun.

"In the midst of this tragedy, prophets appeared among the people and spoke these words, 'YE WOULD NOT GO AS FREE PEOPLE TO ALL THE WORLD WITH THE MESSAGE OF THE KINGDOM. . . . NOW, YE SHALL CARRY IT AS SLAVES.' "

What the evangelist saw confirmed experiences I had even as a young child.

Somewhere in the Soviet Union

In a series of dreams, I saw myself being held captive in Russia.

When I was eight years old I dreamed of a little church with a cross on top of a peaked roof. I opened the door and walked inside. As I did I entered into, for the first time in my life, the presence of God. The little church was only big enough for one person. The approximate dimensions were six feet long, four feet wide and six feet high. The only object inside this little church was one small wooden seat attached to the wall; everything else was cement. There wasn't even a window. Being only eight years old, I didn't know I was in a prison cell.

Twenty years later the Lord spoke to me in a subway car: "I am going to speak to you through a man about your missionary work for me in this world." I decided that instead of traveling to New Jersey to visit my parents I had better go to the meeting at the Calvary Baptist Church, where John Hill from Texas was speaking. When brother Hill began to speak about Christians who lived behind the iron and bamboo curtains, I could actually see, in the spirit, scales falling off my eyes. And I knew that someday I would be serving the Lord inside a communist country.

In 1978, I dreamed I was being held captive in the Soviet Union. I was sitting on a bench in a small but very modern city park. The park was adjacent to the building in which I lived. I was having some real good Christian fellowship with a husband and wife who were good friends of mine. The wife was expecting a baby. In the next sequence of the dream, the husband came walking towards me. He said, "They have taken away our baby at birth." I will never forget the look on his face—grief no tongue could tell. As we embraced, his sorrow became my sorrow. I then momentarily awoke, yet I was still filled with sorrow. I closed my eyes, and now I was sitting on the grass in that same park.

A stranger, whom I recognized as being an American, came over to where I was sitting. I asked her, "Do you have any news from America?" She looked around very suspiciously and replied, "Let's go for a walk. I need to find a drug store." I knew there was one located on a corner a couple of blocks down on the left. She started to walk in that direction, but I didn't go with her because I knew I was not allowed to leave the park. It was obvious she was under a lot of pressure as she nervously walked away. Suddenly, I realized where I was—I was in a large city somewhere in the Soviet Union. I became filled with the Holy Spirit. "The peace of God which surpasses all understanding" flooded my soul (Phil. 4:7). Alleluia!

Russia, God's Servant?

Most of us find it inconceivable that God would use a nation as wicked as the Soviet Union to bring judgment on America or on any nation. The senseless shooting down of the Korean civilian airliner, and the brutal invasion of Afghanistan, are just two examples of its gross iniquity, and how it deserves judgment more than America does. Interestingly enough, the Old Testament prophet Habbakuk felt the same way about God using the Babylonians to judge Israel's southern kingdom. "O Lord, You have appointed them for judgment: O Rock, You have marked them for correction. You are of purer eyes than to behold evil, and cannot look on wickedness. Why do You look on those who deal treacherously, and hold Your tongue when the wicked devours one more righteous than he?" (Hab. 1:12, 13).

Likewise, the Lord through the prophet Jeremiah revealed His plan to send His servant, the king of Babylon, to conquer Jerusalem and the surrounding nations. " 'Behold, I will send and take all the families of the north,' says the Lord, 'and Nebuchadnezzar the king of Babylon, *My servant,* and will bring them against this land, against its inhabitants, and against these nations all around, and will utterly destroy them, and make them an astonishment, a hissing, and perpetual desolations'" (Jer. 25:9, emphasis added).

One hundred and fifty years before the Babylonian captivity, the Lord had already chosen Cyrus, the future gentile king of Persia, to be His "shepherd" and His "anointed" for the purpose of delivering Israel from Babylon, and restoring His people to their land (Isa. 45:1-13).

Necho, a heathen king of Egypt, had emphatically warned Josiah, the King of Judah, "I have not come against you this day, but against the house [Carchemish, a Hittite city] with which I have war; for God commanded me to make haste. Refrain from meddling with God, who is with me, lest He destroy you" (2 Chron. 35:21). Unfortunately, Josiah meddled with God's agent of retribution and was destroyed.

These few scriptural references do not entirely explain God's reasons for using wicked nations to carry out His judgments on other nations that are often not as wicked; they do, at least, shed a little light on God's sovereignty over a cruel, seemingly out-of-control world. For, as Daniel told the Babylonian king Belshazzar on the night he was slain by the conquering Medes and Persians: "The Most High God rules in the kingdom of men, and appoints over it whomever He chooses" (Dan. 5:21).

13
Why Judgment?

What wrong has America committed to deserve such a horrible fate as nuclear devastation, invasion, and having its people shipped out as slave labor? After the Lord had shown me what judgments He is going to send upon America, and had confirmed it through other members of the Body of Christ who had experienced similar revelations, I began to cry out to the Lord, "Why are you sending these terrible judgments upon America?" The answer I received wasn't quite what I expected. If God had attributed His sending judgment to the astronomical number of abortions, divorces, alcoholics, perverts, greedy people and so on, I would have to some extent anticipated it. But God's short answer silenced my questioning. I became dumb before Him as He expressed His reason for sending judgment. The Lord said, "My people are going through the motions, playing church; and they are involved with the World Council of Churches."

The Laodicean Church

God's anger with American Christians can be better understood in light of His message to the Laodicean church in the book of Revelation. They too were lukewarm, going through the motions, playing church. In contrast, God's word to us is forthright, clear, and reliable.

God's message to the Laodicean church was founded on divine authority: "These things says the Amen, the Faithful and True Witness . . ." (Rev. 3:14).

God told them, "I know your works, that you are neither cold nor hot. Because you are lukewarm, and neither cold nor hot, I will spew you out of my mouth" (vv. 15, 16). Yet the Laodiceans were unaware of their own deficiencies, because they were measuring their condition by their own spiritual thermometer instead of Christ's. They thought their temperature was fine. But God told them, "Because you say, 'I am rich, have become wealthy, and have need of nothing'—and do not know that you are wretched, miserable, poor, blind, and naked" (v. 17).

What is the cause of spiritual lukewarmness? How did the Laodiceans come to think they were wealthy when in God's eyes they were poor? Spiritual pride is often the cause of lukewarmness. It deceives us. We perceive ourselves as rich, wealthy and in need of nothing when in reality we are totally bankrupt. Spiritual pride also causes us to look down our noses at other Christians, vainly trying to lift ourselves above their level, finding fault with them while overlooking our own faults. Any criticism of other Christians that issues from a spiritually proud heart is nothing more than a futile, sinful effort to justify ourselves.

God wanted to heal the Laodiceans of this spiritual disease. He desired the very best for them, and all they had to do was accept the Great Physician's advice. He was giving them a word of hope. Not all was lost—He cared for them and cares for us. "I counsel you to buy from Me gold refined in the fire, that you may be rich; and white garments, that you may be clothed, that the shame of your nakedness may not be revealed; and anoint your eyes with salve, that you may see. As many as I love, I rebuke and chasten. Therefore be zealous and repent" (vv. 18, 19). It was out of a heart of love for them that God rebuked His people in Laodicea. He could have let them go their own merry way to destruction, but instead He chose to reveal their sin to them, threaten them with judgment and exhort them to repent.

Not only was God's Word to the Laodicean church directed to the group of believers; it was addressed to the individual members as well. Even though the corporate church was in danger of judgment, each member was ultimately responsible for his relationship to Christ. The opportunity was always there for personal repentance and revival; in any church, restoration must begin with individuals welcoming the presence of the living God into their hearts. He told them, "Behold, I stand at the door and knock. If anyone hears My voice and opens the door, I will come into him, and dine with him, and he with Me" (v. 20).

The message to the church in Laodicea was intended not only to spur them to repentance, but to motivate every lukewarm believer to examine his situation, to inquire whether his wealth consists of gold refined in the fire or whether he is proud but, in God's eyes, wretched, miserable, poor, blind, and naked.

God loves the church in America today just as much as He loved the church in Laodicea. His love for us is behind His warnings, rebukes, and punishment: all are intended to turn our hearts back to Him, to take our eyes off our illusory wealth and focus them on our need for gold refined in the fire. "To him who overcomes I will grant to sit with Me on My throne, as I also overcame and sat down with My Father on His Throne. He who has an ear, let him hear what the Spirit says to the churches" (vv. 21, 22).

Lukewarmness is an inward, sinful, subtle thing that always goes unnoticed by the church. Yet its outward detrimental effect on society, though quite evident, is usually blamed by the church on someone or something else. A lukewarm Church allows ungodliness to permeate any society to the core; thus God's reasoning for severely punishing lukewarm churches as well as the unbelieving societies in which they exist becomes clear. Recall these words from Brother Lambert's prophecy, "Wrath Upon the Land": "THE VILENESS AND THE WICKEDNESS OF MAN HAVE COME UP BEFORE ME AS A STINK IN MY NOSTRILS AND I WILL NOT BE ABLE TO STAY MY HAND ANY LONGER. I AM SICK TO MY STOMACH. THE MOCKERY OF MY WORD IN THE RELIGIOUS SYSTEMS OF AMERICA ARE AN ABOMINATION TO ME. I HAVE COME TO MY BURSTING POINT AND WILL SPEW OUT MY WRATH UPON THE LAND . . ."

Closer to Rebuke

On a radio broadcast of *Moody Presents* entitled "Divine Mercy", November 28, 1982, Dr. George Sweeting, president of Moody Bible Institute, spoke a prophetic word which corresponds to the present condition of the church in America today. "One of the major problems facing the church today is the great number of lukewarm, unenthusiastic followers who fail to stand up and] be counted . . . a cozy, respectable fellowship in a placid city is not good enough—it will not do the job."

Later in his message, Dr. Sweeting commented on the status of the church in North Africa 1200 years ago, and the church in Russia a half century ago. "Saltless and tasteless, it soon was trodden under foot. Feeling no sense of urgency, these churches drifted into death." Dr. Sweeting then compared those churches to the church in America today. "My friend, it is very possible that Christians who are complacent about the ghettos of our cities . . . may be closer to the rebuke of Jesus than all their worldly neighbors who profess no particular spiritual concern."

Ye Would Not Go

Lukewarmness will no doubt smother a church's missionary fire. The overall lack of evangelistic zeal in the American Body of Christ will, if continued, reap tragic events. Recall the prophecy "And God Sent Prophets." "In the midst of this tragedy, prophets appeared among the people and spoke these words, 'Ye would not go as free people to all the world with the message of the kingdom . . . Now, ye shall carry it as slaves.' "

No Stone Unturned

When repentance isn't forthcoming, our God, who is rich in mercy, will administer (short of spewing us out of His mouth) different judgments in an effort to bring us to our senses.

During his 1981 radio interview concerning prophecies of future judgments on America (which included America being invaded by the Soviet Union), John Jackson* was asked, "What is the message the Lord is giving you up till now through these prophecies?" Brother Jackson replied: "During all this time I felt a definite awareness that the Lord was calling His people to repent, that He had given us years of prosperity to draw us to Him, and it did not work in many cases. And because of that He was not going to leave any stone unturned. He is going to allow years that are not as prosperous, and in fact in some cases are destructive, full of calamities, that are depressional in nature; and in this way bring the hearts of America back to Him. That permeated everything. It was though, 'I don't want this to come upon you, but it must come upon you, it must in order for your hearts to turn back to me.'

---

* *John Paul Jackson*, a husband and father, lives in Kansas City, Missouri. He is a member of a local church, and has recently completed his first year of full-time Christian service as an evangelist. In 1981, a Christian radio station, KVTT, Dallas, Texas, taped an interview of John Paul Jackson describing his various prophetic revelations about America. Any prophecy in this book attributed to brother Jackson has been transcribed from his taped radio interview with his permission. If you wish to obtain additional information concerning John Paul Jackson's prophecies, please contact LAMP & OIL ministries, Kansas City, Missouri.

"Sometimes this is the only way that we can turn to the Lord, and many of us only turn to God during crisis situations. And it's a shame God has to bring us to that point before we will seek the face of the Lord."

The Kremlin

God will dispatch Russia to conquer America in order to turn the hearts of His people toward Him.

Just prior to the 1980 "Washington for Jesus" rally, Mike Parks, who at the time was caring for a parapalegic and preaching the Gospel on the streets of Portland, Oregon, told me of a vision he had of the Kremlin. He described the Kremlin's appearance as huge and massive, its towers stretching far above him. Its ominous presence caused him to cry out to the Lord "Why?" The Lord answered him, "So that My people will look up."

The World Council of Churches

God's other reason for sending judgment on America is the twenty-eight American Christian denominations and parachurch groups that are members of the World Council of Churches (WCC). The WCC is an international religious organization consisting of Christian denominations from all over the world. However, its financial backing and philosophical espousing of communist causes are anything but Christian. There are also thirty-two American church bodies that are involved with the WCC via the National Council of Churches of Christ (NCCC). Most of these church groups independently belong to the WCC as well. The controversial, exclusively American NCCC, though not an official member of the WCC, does send observers to their meetings. Through its missionary arm, the Church World Service, the NCCC has continued to work hand in hand with the WCC on a variety of international relief and development projects.

The suspect activities of the WCC have been adequately exposed by a substantial number of Christian treatises; however, for the sake of those who have not read or heard of the WCC's incompatibility with Christianity, I will briefly state a few examples of its non-Christian witness. The WCC's financial assistance of the United Revolutionary Directorate (D.R.U.), a united communist front in El Salvador, is nothing new; the WCC also supplied Fidel Castro's material needs.

The April 26, 1981, Newark (New Jersey) *Star Ledger* reported that the El Salvadorian government had captured rebel documents which revealed that "Angel V. Peiro, assistant secretary for Latin America of the Geneva-based WCC, instructed his representative in El Salvador to make available to CESHA $500,000 in donations."[4] CESHA, the Council for Humanitarian Assistance, is a phony religious and social agency set up to aid the communist guerillas in El Salvador. "The CESHA contact was identified as Marta Benavides. The D.R.U. document identifies "comrade" Benavides as a member of El Salvador's Communist Party."[5]

The WCC, through a special fund established by its Program to Combat Racism (PCR), has unashamedly continued to openly dole out funds to communist revolutionaries who are fighting to overthrow the predominantly white governments of Africa. Over the past twelve years the PCR has contributed $12.5 million to communist insurgents in Nambia, Angola and Zimbabwe.[6] In 1978, the PCR's special fund contributed $85,000 to the Patriotic Front of Zimbabwe (Rhodesia), a communist group which eventually fought its way to power. The money could have been distributed in Zimbabwe through a Christian agency, the Salvation Army, but it wasn't. This kind of procedure is typical of the WCC. In 1979 an amendment was proposed to the WCC's governing central committee that the special PCR fund should make use "wherever possible of indigenous Christian agencies to deliver the humanitarian services desired."[7] The amendment was overwhelmingly defeated. Since 1978 the Salvation Army, the Presbyterian Church of Ireland and a small German Lutheran Church have suspended their membership in the WCC.

The WCC has never denied its funding of communist causes, but has continually justified its support by asserting the money is "to be used for humanitarian activities."[8] Now if you give a communist who is fighting a revolution money to buy food, this will leave him with more money to buy guns. This is like saying, "I didn't let that mad dog out of the cage; all I did was open the door." Does the WCC really expect us to be so naive or are they really that deceived? The WCC's supposedly humanitarian grants are bestowed upon communist guerillas "without control of the manner in which they are spent."[9] Since 1971, the WCC has said it does not "pass judgment on those victims of racism who are driven to violence as the only way left to them to redress grievances."[10] Meanwhile, American Christians who are involved with the World Council of Churches participate in killing more and more innocent people—all in the name of Jesus.

The vast majority of church delegates from the communist countries to the WCC are government-appointed wolves in sheep's clothing, or Christians who, after much hideous torture, have denied their faith and subsequently praise the hand that beat them. For the sake of ecumenism, many of the Western nations and Third World delegates tend to accommodate their communist counterparts, while others, in total agreement with the communist representatives, advocate "liberation theology," a Marxist brand of Christianity that strives "to set at liberty those who are oppressed" through violent revolution (Luke 4:18). This is why in 1983, during the WCC's general assembly (which meets every eight years), in Vancouver, Canada, hardly a murmur was heard over the WCC's continued funding of the South West Africa Peoples Organization (SWAPO), a communist guerilla movement which is presently fighting to overthrow the government of South West Africa (Namibia). This is also why official statements drawn up by that assembly praised "the life-affirming achievements" of the Nicaraguan communist regime,[11] called for a greater awareness of the Palestinians' "urgent and just" cause,[12] and vigorously accused the United States of trying to "destabilize the Nicaraguan government, renew international support for Guatemala's violent military regimes, resist the forces of historic change in El Salvador and militarize Honduras."[13] In keeping in line with past rhetoric, not one word came forth to condemn the Soviet Union's butchery in Afghanistan, or the several thousand Christian brethren verified to be rotting in communist jails (Richard Wurmbrand, head of Jesus to the Communist World, believes that the number of Christians in communist prisons is much higher.)

The American Body of Christ's relationship to the WCC, in conjunction with its lukewarm state, is ample cause for God to judge His church in America.

Secondary Cause

A society in which a lukewarm church exists will become increasingly more and more wicked and thus ripen itself for judgment.

Freedom Will No Longer Ring

If we as a nation will not serve the Lord, then America will no longer be a free and sovereign land.

I awoke one morning singing these words in my spirit:

> My country 'tis of thee,
> Sweet land of liberty,
>   Of thee I sing.
> Land where my fathers died,
> Land of the Pilgrims' pride,
> From every mountain side,
>   Let freedom ring.
> (Samuel Francis Smith, 1808-1897)

As I sang, the burden of the Lord overwhelmed me and I received this revelation: "If this country isn't of Thee (God), then freedom will no longer ring." My entire being began to ache and sob. Words inadequately describe how I felt at that moment. It was as if Jesus were weeping over America through me. Oh, how the Lord yearns and tenderly pleads for the American people to worship and serve Him; but if we choose not to, then those freedoms that He has graciously bestowed upon us will be taken away.

The Banner

In 1974 I beheld in a vision a segment of America's secular population rioting in the street.

I saw a hostile street mob. And far off in the distance I could also see smoke spiraling upward. This angry bunch comprised Americans of all races: black, Hispanic and white. And although I could not hear what they were yelling, I could actually see hatred drip from one black man's face like water. His fist was raised in the air as he stood in the forefront of a small but enraged crowd who were screaming violently at a banner that was stretched high across the street. The banner was the kind you would normally see at a political rally, the only difference being it was old and heavily frayed around the edges. Otherwise it was in good shape. The banner bore this inscription: *76 Reagan 76.*

I knew Ronald Reagan was running against President Ford for the Republican party's nomination for president, but for many years I could not comprehend the significance of the vision, especially the frayed banner with its inscription. I earnestly sought the Lord for the meaning of this vision, and in the latter part of 1983 He showed me that the banner represented our nation's two-hundred-year Christian heritage, thus the 76 inscribed on the banner, and the banner's old and frayed appearance. The Lord revealed to me that the people in the vision were rebelling against the Christian principles and ideals·this nation had been founded upon. The Lord also showed me that President Reagan's name was inscribed on the banner because he, more than any other president in recent history, has epitomized those Christian values.

I fear that if this should come to pass, it would be a sign that America's secular society in general will have totally rejected the Gospel. Were this to happen, much havoc and chaos would be created throughout our nation. Those who would participate in this rebellion against the God-appointed "governing authorities" would only "bring judgment on themselves" (Rom. 13:1, 2).

Conclusion

The combination of the American Christian church being lukewarm in spirit and "unequally yoked together with unbelievers [the WCC]" (2 Cor. 6:14) has incited the American people to rebel against our country's godly heritage, and is sufficient reason for God to mete out His just recompense upon our entire nation.

A lukewarm church alone would justify God's judgment of America. Add to that the churches' involvement with the WCC and the American public's rejection of the Gospel, and America will arrive at the same tragic destination as Israel and so many other nations. "For three transgressions of Israel and for four, I will not turn away its punishment" (Amos 2:6).

14
How Soon?

Our nation's time of grace is almost up. God will not wait until after the Rapture or during the Great Tribulation to judge America. We are quickly approaching the day when these horrendous judgments will suddenly fall upon our land. I'm not setting dates, but I believe the Lord is saying, "Soon, very soon."

Digital Watch

Kay Fowler beheld a vision of America on borrowed time.

"In the past, I've seen a watch, it's a digital watch. And it's zero hours, zero minutes, and zero seconds. As I'm looking at this watch the seconds begin to move forward—one, two, three seconds. And then it approaches 59 seconds; and then it moves into minutes. As it approaches 60 minutes, the numbers continue counting up—61, 62, 63 minutes. Therefore the Lord has shown that we are in the last hour. He's not going to give us another hour; only a few minutes. Indeed, America is on borrowed time."

Throes of Judgment

America has begun to experience the type of judgments that will result in its downfall. The Lord, after showing me many cataclysmic events that are yet to take place in this nation, in October 1981 informed me that He desired to commune with me further on this matter. After a few days of wondering what the Lord was going to say, I earnestly began to seek the Lord with fasting and prayer. And as I was praying, God spoke to my heart something I will never forget. He said, "We are entering the throes of judgment." I became deeply grieved for America, realizing our nation is quickly approaching the day when God shall send terrible judgments upon our land to overthrow us. I also became keenly aware that God had already visited our nation with lesser types of judgment in an effort to draw us back to himself before it's too late. It's almost too late.

The Stump and the Bear

Kay Fowler saw in a vision that America, like a tree, would soon be cut down.

"Early one morning I saw in a vision the stump of an old tree that had been cut down, and right behind it there was a big bear. And the bear was approaching the stump. I asked the Lord what he was showing me. And He gave me the scripture from the book of Luke, chapter thirteen, verses six to nine, KJV. 'A certain man had a fig tree planted in his vineyard; and he came and sought fruit thereon, and found none. Then said he unto the dresser of his vineyard, "Behold, these three years I come seeking fruit on this fig tree, and find none: cut it down; why cumbereth it the ground?" And he answering said unto him, "Lord, let it alone this year also, till I shall dig about it, and dung it: and if it bear fruit, well: and if not, then after that thou shall cut it down." 'I know the stump of this tree represents America, and Russia is known as the bear."

Three Witnesses and Tulip Seeds

Because of a series of dreams in 1979 and 1980, Kay Fowler sensed that without fervent intercession, America would be severely judged within two or three years.

"In June of 1979, the Lord sent me in a dream three witnesses. They stood before me and said: 'Kay, have you heard, in one year judgment will come upon America?' this first one spoke. The second spoke, 'Yes, have you heard in one year judgment will be upon America?' And the third one said, 'Yes, in one year judgment will be upon America.' Now as I pondered upon this I thought, 'In one year America will surely be under judgment.'

"Now I've not only seen judgment to be that of war but in other forms such as drought. I've seen the farming land all up and down this area sold because of the drought and also the bad economic condition we are in. In 1980, I saw myself in a community with my hands cupped to my mouth yelling: 'Water will become precious! Water will become precious!' And I believe that we can all see that this has become a reality all across our nation. And I think there are many who felt as I did that the eruption of Mount St. Helens was the beginning of judgment, and a sign to this country that perilous times are ahead.

"So after much more prayer for an understanding of the three witnesses, I could see one year was given to each; hence, three years. As for further confirmation I received a dream.

"Early in 1980 I received a dream concerning some tulips. My grandmother had planted some red tulips in my yard, and she had planted the seeds instead of the bulbs. I replied to her, 'What a shame, for I won't be here when they bloom, for I'll be hid away.' So I called the nursery to inquire about the tulip seeds, and when they would bloom. I was told from two to three years. I'm not going to give a projection of time. I don't want to dwell on a time piece, or prophesy a date. For I know many intercessors are on their knees before the Lord. And I know that prayer and fasting has postponed judgment in times past. We are pleading day by day with God for more time."

15
What Shall We Do?

Today, the destiny of America hangs in the balance. Will God continue to send judgments until America is eventually overthrown, or will America repent and be spared God's worst judgments? I am convinced the decisions made in the near future by the Christians in America will ultimately determine the fate of this nation. If the church chooses to submit itself to the Lordship of Jesus Christ, then not only will the church be revived, but multitudes of heathens in America and around the world will be saved, and God will relent and spare us the fearful judgments He plans to send upon America.

As a national church we have exhausted every method and means to generate revival in our midst and throughout the land. Our futile attempts have brought us to the end of the line; like the Ninevites and the church at Laodicea, we have only two options—repent or perish!

The Ninevites, having heard Jonah's judgment message "Yet forty days and Nineveh shall be overthrown," believed God (Jon. 3:4, 5). Nineveh's thorough repentance commanded God's attention and stayed His hand of wrath.

The church at Laodicea heard the Spirit of the Lord say to them, "I will spew you out of My mouth" (Rev. 3:16). It would be reasonable to assume that the first-century Laodicean church responded favorably to the Spirit's prophetic warning spoken through John, for the city of Laodicea prospered and existed well into the twelfth century.

The church in America must also repent of going through the motions—of playing church, of being lukewarm, if our nation is to be spared God's judgments and to experience revival.

God has convicted me of the utter sinfulness of my own lukewarm condition, and I have repented of it. During a service at our First Christian Assembly in Plainfield, New Jersey, our pastor, Fran Huber, asked the congregation to hold hands and pretend that the person standing next to us was a Christian of a different persuasion, such as Messianic Jew, Catholic, Episcopalian, or Southern Baptist. Then, as he began to minister to the church on how our various doctrinal differences nonessential to salvation have divided the Body of Christ, destroying the oneness Jesus intended us to have, I realized that the reason we Christians look down on others is so that we can try to exalt ourselves above them. I clearly understood that my disagreements with other Christians over doctrines nonessential to salvation had nothing to do with establishing the truth of God's Word, but only enhancing my own self-righteousness at their expense. At this point, I began to experience the terrible bitter agony of being separated from my Christian brothers, especially those with whom I had these doctrinal differences. It was as if I had awakened and discovered that a part of my body was missing. I felt so incomplete, so helpless, so undone. In numbed astonishment I sat there covered with the ashes of pride, when from deep within my spirit a thought that had been surpressed far too long suddenly burst into my conscience: "I need my Presbyterian brother." I then vividly saw the face of a Holiness brother whom I had thought less of because of his biblical views nonessential to salvation; I needed him too! For several days a godly sorrow shrouded my soul as I confessed my sin to my brothers and sisters, and asked forgiveness from those whom I had wronged.

Jesus prayed that all those who would believe on Him for salvation would be one (John 17:20-23). There cannot be any significant revival in America or any place else until Christians manifest the spiritual reality of the oneness of Christ's Body and become the answer to Jesus' prayer. The early church in Jerusalem "had all things in common" because they had Jesus in common (Acts 2:44). That is why they had revival. Brothers and sisters, if the American church is to have revival, if you and I are to be greatly used by God, then we must first repent of our lukewarmness, which includes any ill treatment of our brethren; then, in spite of our nonessential doctrinal differences, we must unite as the Body of Christ. Otherwise, we shall continue to divide Christ's Body, and grieve the heart of God until our nation is overthrown in judgment.

I am not saying that in order to attain Christian unity we all must join the same denomination, or worship in the same manner, or agree on doctrines nonessential to salvation; but it is imperative that we put into practice the advice given to the rival factions within the Corinthian church by the apostle Paul: "There should be no schism in the body, but . . . the members should have the same care for one another" (1 Cor. 12:25).

The late Paul E. Billheimer wrote an excellent book on Christian unity entitled *Love Covers.* I highly recommend it.

"If My People"

Shortly after the temple was built, when Israel was at its zenith, the Lord, knowing the rebelliousness of His people, made known His will to Solomon concerning their eventual falling away. "If My people who are called by My name will humble themselves, and pray and seek My face, and turn from their wicked ways, then I will hear from heaven, and will forgive their sin and heal their land" (2 Chron. 7:14).

Humbling ourselves, praying, seeking His face, and forsaking our wicked ways are all prerequisites, along with the blood of Jesus, for God hearing our prayers, forgiving our sins and healing our land. "If My people," means the choice is the Christians'. However, we don't have to obey God; we can stubbornly go our own way and suffer the consequences as Israel did.

Brothers and sisters, time is running out; catastrophic judgments are coming. Yet the Lord still pleads with the American church, as He did with Israel when they had gone astray and were facing judgment. The Lord spoke to His people through the prophet Jeremiah, "Behold, I am fashioning a disaster and devising a plan against you. *Return now every one* from his evil way, and make your ways and your doings good" (Jer. 18:11, emphasis added). As I concluded proclaiming the message of America's soon coming judgment at a Gospel street meeting, the Lord made a similar appeal through me to the American brethren, announcing, "Be prepared to meet thy God in judgment and calamity. Return unto Me, My people; O return unto Me!"

What shall we do? If the Church does not repent, America will fall. Therefore, knowing both the love and severity of God, and realizing the grave consequences America is presently facing, we, the Body of Christ, ought to heed God's warning and return to Him in repentance.

In his book *America Is Too Young To Die*,[14] evangelist Leonard Ravenhill emphasized the urgent need for repentance in the Church as the only means of national restoration. "I think that we shall have to be corrected by the rod! I fear at times that the Nation will suffer for the sin of the Church rather than the Church suffer for the sin of the Nation. The Church needs to repent, to shed her worldliness. The preachers need to repent first. Let the priests, the ministers of the Lord, weep before the barren altars, weep over the lost, unloved, unsought millions, weep that there is not a pillar of fire over the sanctuary to say that God is in residence. He stands at the door. Will He wait much longer? Let the Church live again with holy passion and America will be re-born. There is no other door of hope."

Your Decision. In the Scriptures, Paul admonished the Corinthians to quickly separate and cleanse themselves from all ungodly relationships. This advice also applies to any Christian who belongs to or participates in the *work* of the WCC. "Do not be unequally yoked together with unbelievers. For what fellowship has righteousness with lawlessness? And what communion has light with darkness? And what accord has Christ with Belial? Or what part has a believer with an unbeliever? And what agreement has the temple of God with idols? For you are the temple of the living God. As God has said: 'I will dwell in them and walk among them. I will be their God, and they shall be My people.' Therefore 'Come out from among them and be separate,' says the Lord. 'Do not touch what is unclean, and I will receive you. I will be a Father to you, and you shall be My sons and daughters,' says the Lord Almighty. Therefore, having these promises, beloved, let us cleanse ourselves from all filthiness of the flesh and spirit, perfecting holiness in the fear of God" (2 Cor. 6:14-18; 7:1).

If American Christianity's involvement in the WCC is part of God's reason for judging our nation, then it is imperative that we believers "come out from among them." Otherwise, God will not spare our land, nor the Church within it.

Granted, there are a few Christians, such as David du Plessis, who have a legitimate ministry as a witness for Christ to the WCC (du Plessis has attended all six WCC general assemblies). I do not consider these Christians "unequally yoked" with the WCC, and would not encourage them to leave unless God directed them to do so.

A revived Church would quickly sever its ties with the WCC. Even so, as a brother in Christ, I exhort the Christian leadership, local pastors and all believers of the various twenty-eight Christian denominations and parachurch organizations who are joined to the WCC to unite in an effort to withdraw their respective church memberships, as did the Salvation Army, as part of the prerequisite of turning from our wicked ways. I also exhort the NCCC and other church groups to likewise discontinue their support of the WCC.

What I have said is radical. You are probably asking yourself, "Why must I take such an extreme step?" My answer to you is: one way or the other God is going to convince His people in America to separate themselves from the WCC. One way for them would be to heed God's warning and leave *now!* The other way, the way of judgment, would also induce God's people to depart from the WCC, but God wants to spare us this misery.

The Lord does not want you to belong to or support the World Council of Churches. There are plenty of Christian ministries that need your help. Brothers and sisters, it is your decision, but your blood will not be upon my hands.

Prayer

Besides repenting of our lukewarmness, and coming out of the WCC, God is calling the American church to fulfill its greatest privilege and most important duty—to pray. Praying for one's nation, especially its leaders, is every Christian's responsibility. Paul told Timothy "that supplications, prayers, intercessions, and giving of thanks be made for all men, for kings and all who are in authority, that we may lead a quiet and peaceable life in all godliness and reverence" (1 Tim. 2:1, 2).

Moses' intercession averted God's destruction of Israel when they worshiped idols while Moses was busy receiving the Ten Commandments (Exod. 32:10-14). Two other instances when God determined to destroy Israel are found in Numbers 14:11-24 and 2 Samuel. But again intercession prevented annihilation.

God notified Habakkuk that He was dispatching the awesome Babylonian army as a judgment upon his native land, Judah. Due to the certainty of that judgment, Habakkuk pleaded with God for restoration and mercy: "Oh Lord, I have heard your speech and was afraid; O Lord, revive Your work in the midst of the years! In the midst of the years make it known; in wrath remember mercy" (Hab. 3:2).

Take Hold of God

The late W.C. Moore (1890-1980), founder and former editor of *The Herald of His Coming*, a Christian publication trumpeting the call to repentance and revival, wrote an article entitled "The Gates of Hell Shall Not Prevail"[15] stressing the necessity of a revived Church as the only insurance against God sending foreign invaders as judgment upon the church in America (as well as upon the entire nation). He wrote:

> Halt! Hands Up! With a gun pointing in our face, we don't argue or dillydally—we put up our hands! Let us, O Let us, as a nation, get down on our knees—before we are crushed under the cruel heel of an invading oppressor!
>
> God's moment is now! "NOW is the accepted time: behold, NOW is the day of salvation" (2 Cor. 6:2) I'd far, far rather get wholeheartedly in earnest, in importunate prayer for Revival NOW—than to cry my heart out from a dismal dungeon, as some have done. I'd rather fast and pray NOW—

by choice—than to starve by necessity in a conqueror's slave camp. Have not thousands in recent years suffered and died in such camps?

"Woe to them that are at ease in Zion!" (read Amos 6:1-7). I had rather stir up myself (Isa. 64:7) NOW, and take hold of God for Revival, and not let Him go till He answers (Gen. 32:24-28)—than to loiter around, and take things easy, and enjoy myself—while a cunning enemy "takes over" in our beloved land, and sends thousands of us to foreign slave camps—where, without mercy, we will be tortured, mistreated, and worked to death!

Join with me, and with others, in definite and desperate agreement (Matt. 18:19)—that God will speedily (Luke 18:1-8)—send a New Testament, Holy Ghost Revival to this Wicked Nation!

Where Are The Volunteers for God's Army of Prayer Warriors?

In a letter to *The Herald of His Coming*,[16] a minister called the American Christians to pray for America.

"I have just completed a seven-week prayer vigil, from two to six hours daily, in the park where I formerly ministered to hippies. From the very beginning the Lord has shown me that America is facing judgment, and that unless we His people PRAY NOW we shall regretfully pay later. I asked for confirmation of what He was showing me, and began receiving it immediately. First I received a letter from a former missionary sister in another state.

She told me that the Lord has been giving her much revelation through the night hours and often during the day concerning judgment that America is facing, and that He is calling upon His people to fervently pray. In her latest letter she writes: 'PLEASE PRAY, PRAY FOR OUR NATION . . . A STORM IS COMING AND WHO WILL BE ABLE TO STAND? . . .'

"America is in danger and it will take an army of Christian prayer warriors to either avert or lessen the calamity . . .

"Thank God for those prayer warriors and prayer groups that are interceding before God's Throne night and day for this nation and the nations of the world. But the fact remains that most of the Body of professing believers are leading careless, prayerless, apathetic, world-conforming, lukewarm lives. And if they do pray they are weak, lethargic 'Now-I-lay-me-down-to-sleep' type of prayers.

"But this is no time to be sleeping. NOW IT IS HIGH TIME WE AWAKE AND PUT OFF THE WORKS OF DARKNESS . . .

"Conformed to the world, many believers have become lovers of pleasure more than lovers of God, and the Lord said it would be exactly this way in these last days (2 Tim. 3;4). The Lord said to His disciples, 'Could ye not watch with Me one hour?' (Matt. 26:40). From many the answer today would be, 'Some other time, Lord. There's a special on TV I've just got to see . . .'

"WHERE ARE THE VOLUNTEERS FOR GOD'S ARMY OF PRAYER WARRIORS? WHERE ARE THEY TO BE FOUND?"

Battle of Britain

Oppressed by their enemies, the Israelites would pray before or during a battle and God would give them the victory. (2 Kings 19:1-19; 2 Sam. 5:18-25; 2 Chron. 20:1-27). Likewise, the Battle of Britain is a modern-day example of the churches' faith in God's delivering power in time of national crisis.

The students and faculty of Wales Bible College devoted themselves to continual fasting and prayer throughout the duration of World War II, especially during the larger, more decisive conflicts. And perhaps there is no greater example of effective intercessory prayer than what was wrought by this Christian school during the Battle of Britain.

The German Luftwaffe (air force) had suffered heavy losses while trying to soften up the British Isles for invasion, so much so that Germany finally turned its mighty war machine elsewhere. What stopped the German onslaught? Was it the small Royal Air Force?

Rees Howells, founder and president of Wales Bible College, wrote in his prayer journal concerning intercession made for London and the King and Queen of England during the height of the battle.

> Sept. 11th. There have been so many places bombed in London, even Buckingham Palace has been touched. I was burdened to pray for the King and Queen. I believe our prayer will be answered. I am just watching how God will take hold of the enemy.
>
> Sept. 12th. We prayed last night that London would be defended and that the enemy would fail to break through and

> God answered prayer. If we can get protection for our properties, why not get protection for the country. What wonderful days these are.[17]

What did their earnest intercession accomplish? On September 15th, the day Mr. Churchill in his war memorial called the "culminating date," the German Luftwaffe, with victory almost in grasp, suddenly retreated back to Germany for no apparent reason.

Norman Grubb, in *Rees Howells Intercessor*,[18] wrote:

> After the war, Air Chief Marshal Lord Dowding, Commander-in-Chief of Fighter Command in the Battle of Britain made this significant comment: "Even during the battle one realized from day to day how much external support was coming in. At the end of the battle one had the sort of feeling that there had been some special Divine Intervention to alter some sequence of events which would otherwise have occurred."

In her book *Tell No Man*, Adela Rogers St. John related how Lord Dowding at a banquet told of angels flying the airplanes of pilots who had been killed during the Battle of Britain. The crew members of one plane actually "saw a figure at the controls" after their pilot had been killed. Miraculously, "the plane kept on flying and fighting."[19]

During a Christian talk show on which Billy Graham was discussing his book *Angels*, another one of the guests told a story about a German fighter pilot.

During the Battle of Britain he saw a number of huge angels with drawn swords surrounding the British aircraft. He was terrified, especially when his plane began to malfunction. He was shot down, but lived to tell the story.

God would not only have Christians praying for the nation, but also for one another and for the Church as a whole.

In each one of his epistles, the apostle Paul displayed a genuine intercessory concern for those to whom he had written, regardless of doctrinal heresy or known sin.

Spare Your People

After God confronted Joel with a description of foreign troops invading Judah, his homeland, Joel not only called the nation to repentance, but exhorted the priests to intercede for God's disobedient people as well.

> Let the priests, who minister to the Lord, weep between the porch and the altar; let them say, "Spare Your people, O Lord, and do not give Your heritage to reproach, that the nations should rule over them. Why should they say among the peoples, "Where is their God?" (Joel 2:17).

As I read the prophecy of Joel, the words "Spare Your people" gripped my attention. They became enlarged upon the page, as if they had been placed under a magnifying glass. The presence of the Lord, like dew permeating the air, filled the room. I could actually feel moisture on my skin. The Lord was standing inside the front doorway of the house. All I could say to Him (in my spirit) was what He had just placed upon my heart: "Spare Your people." The Lord then began to move towards me. His eyes, being the only physical characteristic I could discern, were extremely swollen from excessive weeping, yet He continued to weep. I could hear His relentless whimpering sobs as He drew near. The heartbroken Christ passed by where I stood, proceeded into the kitchen and out the back door of the house. As His presence began to recede, I was made to understand that He was unhappily and ever so reluctantly on His way to judge His church in America. There was no joy in God's heart, only sorrow. He didn't want to do it, but He had to. Judgment was required, and there didn't seem to be any recourse. Yet He had paused to hear my intercession, or should I say the intercessory burden He himself had placed upon my heart.

Though Jesus treads the mournful path that inevitably leads to judgment of His church in America, He is, at this present time, willing to receive intercession for His church. For our Lord's burden is to spare His people, not judge them.

Jesus and the Holy Spirit are interceding for the American Body of Christ and for the nation to repent and experience revival instead of judgment. Let us do likewise.

Conclusion. God is willing to spare His people along with this nation. However, if the fruits of repentance are not visible in the American church, judgment will come. If a holy life does not become the criterion for spiritual maturity, as opposed to material wealth, spiritual gifts, etc.; if the prayer meeting does not become the predominant activity on church calendars; if Christian love does not spread across denominational lines and between independent churches; if the Lord's burden for lost, dying, hell-bound souls remains absent from our consciences—judgment will come. If we refuse to repent of our lukewarm attitudes and behavior, and fail to forsake our unholy alliances, then there can be no revival—only judgment, swift and sure. God will judge His church along with this nation. He will send nuclear warheads to waste our cities. He will order communist troops to march through the land. Americans will be killed, imprisoned, or carried away as slaves at His instructions. Our freedoms—gone. Our hopes—dashed. Our plans—shattered. Judgment will have come. It could be avoided, but we won't listen; or will we?

16
If Judgment Comes

If God, because of the unrepented wickedness in the land, decides to overthrow America, will that be the end of her, or will she rise again to her former greatness and stature? Scripturally speaking, this question is difficult to answer since there is no direct reference to America in the Bible. There are, however, a number of scriptural examples of God being merciful in the midst of judgment.

The Flood. God, at one time, contemplated annihilating the entire human race. In the days of Noah, "the Lord saw that the wickedness of man was great in the earth, and that every intent of the thoughts of his heart was only evil continually" (Gen. 6:5). God regretted creating mankind, and painfully decided to terminate His creation. He said, "I will destroy man" (v. 7). But as God surveyed the actions and attitudes of all people, "Noah found grace in the eyes of the Lord" (v. 8). And the Lord spared Noah, "a just man" (v. 9), and his family, thereby preserving a remnant, in hope that mankind would once again serve the Creator.

Israel. God would threaten Israel with foreign invasion as a means of bringing them to repentance. If that didn't work He sent the invaders to further persuade them to forsake their sins.

He did not desire to permanently punish His people, but to chastise them in order to draw them back to himself. When their hearts turned from their transgressions unto the Lord, the Lord gave them deliverance from their enemies. Unfortunately, Israel repeated this process time and time again. "Thus they were defiled by their own works, and played the harlot by their own deeds. Therefore the wrath of the Lord was kindled against His people, so that He abhorred His own inheritance. And He gave them into the hand of the Gentile, and those who hated them ruled over them. Their enemies also oppressed them, and they were brought into subjection under their hand. Many times He delivered them; but they rebelled against Him by their counsel, and were brought low for their iniquity. Nevertheless He regarded their affliction, when He heard their cry; and for their sake He remembered His covenant, and relented according to the multitude of His mercies" (Ps. 106:39-45).

The fact that the nation of Israel exists today is one of the greatest proofs of God's benevolent attitude, merciful treatment and genuine love towards mankind, even in the midst of judgment. I sense that God will deal with America, especially the church, in the same fashion; if the future judgments described in this book are sent upon this nation, then America, and the Body of Christ in particular, like Israel, will be severely chastised but not utterly cast down.

George Washington's Vision

America has experienced both prosperity and adversity. Two bloody conflicts have been fought on American soul—the Revolutionary War and the Civil War. But except for the three unsuccessful invasion attempts by the British forces during the War of 1812, which included the burning of Washington, D.C., our nation has never known the terror of foreign invaders.

In the winter of 1777, the father of our country, George Washington, beheld a unique vision at Valley Forge that encompassed a substantial portion of America's future history.

After seeing the vision of America's future, Washington recounted the event to Anthony Sherman, an officer in the Continental Army at Valley Forge. Eighty-two years later, at the age of ninety-nine, Anthony Sherman was the only person alive to know of the vision. On July 4, 1859, he repeated Washington's vision to Wesely Bradshaw, publisher of *The National Tribune*. The story of the occurrence and the content of this vision was first published in the American war veterans' paper, *The National Tribune*, in 1880. The paper is now known as the *Stars and Stripes*. The vision account was reprinted by the *Stars and Stripes* on December 21, 1950 and has subsequently appeared in various publications.[20]

Washington's vision is composed of three great perils, the first being the then current Revolutionary War and its eventual outcome; the second was the future Civil War (Washington actually saw in the vision American fighting American over the issue of slavery); the third great and most fearful peril depicted a future invasion of troops from Europe, Asia and

Africa in which America was overcome but eventually regained its independence.

The Third Peril

"Again I heard the mysterious voice saying, 'Son of the Republic, look and learn.' At this the dark, shadowy angel placed a trumpet to his mouth, and blew three distinct blasts; and taking water from the ocean, he sprinkled it upon Europe, Asia and Africa.

"Then my eyes beheld a fearful scene. From each of these continents arose thick black clouds that were soon joined into one. And throughout this mass there gleamed a dark red light by which I saw hordes of armed men. These men, moving with the cloud, marched by land and sailed by sea to America, which country was enveloped in the volume of the cloud. And I dimly saw these vast armies devastate the whole country and burn the villages, towns and cities which I had seen springing up.

"As my ears listened to the thundering of the cannon, clashing of swords, and the shouts and cries of swords, and the shouts and cries of millions in mortal combat, I again heard the mysterious voice saying, 'Son of the Republic, look and learn.' When this voice had ceased, the dark shadowy angel placed his trumpet once more to his mouth, and blew a long and fearful blast.

Help From Above

"Instantly a light as of a thousand suns shone down from above me, and pierced and broke into fragments the dark cloud which enveloped America. At the same moment the angel upon whose head still shone the word 'Union,' and who bore our national flag in one hand and a sword in the other, descended from the heavens attended by legions of white spirits. These immediately joined the inhabitants of America, who I perceived were well-nigh overcome, but who immediately taking courage again, closed up their broken ranks and renewed the battle.

"Again, amid the fearful noise of the conflict I heard the mysterious voice saying, 'Son of the Republic, look and learn.' As the voice ceased, the shadowy angel for the last time dipped water from the ocean and sprinkled it upon America. Instantly the dark cloud rolled back, together with the armies it had brought, leaving the inhabitants of the land victorious.

"Then once more, I beheld the villages, towns and cities springing up where I had seen them before, while the bright angel, planting the azure standard he had brought in the midst of the them, cried with a loud voice: 'While the stars remain, and the heavens send down dew upon the earth, so long shall the Union last.' And taking from his brow the crown on which blazoned the word 'Union', he placed it upon the Standard while the people, kneeling down said, 'Amen.'

America's Destiny

"The scene instantly began to fade and dissolve, and I at last saw nothing but the rising, curling vapor I at first beheld. This also disappeared, and I found myself once more gazing upon the mysterious visitor, who, in the same voice I had heard before said, 'Son of the Republic, what you have seen is thus interpreted: Three great perils will come upon the Republic. The most fearful for her is the third. But the whole world united shall not prevail against her. Let every child of the Republic learn to live for his God, his land and Union.' With these words the vision vanished, and I started from my seat and felt that I had seen a vision wherein had been shown to me the birth, the progress, and destiny of the United States.' "

"Such, my friends," the venerable narrator concluded, "were the words I heard from Washington's own lips, and America will do well to profit by them."

In confirmation of George Washington's vision of America's future invasion and ensuing restoration, John Jackson, 203 years later, witnessed a similar vision.

We Will Be Victorious![21]

"I was looking down upon the United States as I would a map. I saw many cities in the United States erupt with a flash that to me signified great explosions. A verse came to me at this time that is found in Zephaniah 1:16, that this was as 'a day of the trumpet, and an alarm against the fenced cities and against their high towers.'

"At this time . . . the Lord is going to provide, but on the surface this looks so shaky that I don't want the people to hear this to get anything other than the Lord will see His people through this time. But what I saw was that the flashes were a limited exchanging of bombs. I don't know whether they were nuclear weapons or not, but there was a limited exchange of bombs, and that we had been invaded by Russia: literally and physically invaded by Russia. And that it will appear through this invasion, because it will totally catch us by surprise, that we had lost the war. But God told me and revealed to me that He will supernaturally take charge, and when we have given up hope then He will come in and rescue this land, and we will be victorious. WE WILL BE VICTORIOUS! I cannot emphasize that enough. But at the same time the Lord was preparing me, because during this time it will not be a pretty sight; it will not be fun and games. The Lord is letting us know that we're going to go through in the coming years and months some tumultuous times; that without His help we would perish. During this time, I didn't see it but I knew in my spirit that Israel was also being invaded [Ezek. 38, 39], and I also knew that Russia had waited to invade us until a time when two things were happening: one, they felt we were near internal collapse; and two, we were nearing a break where we were starting to catch up with them in military strength and might, and before that was going to take place they were going to strike while they felt they still had the upper hand; but our upper hand is God. And our hearts will be turned toward him during that time.

Map of Europe

"I also saw toward the end of this vision as a map the countries of Europe. And they were very dark, and I saw a large power springing up, and I saw strength emanating from this power. I did not see a man or an individual. I just saw and knew what I was beholding was power. At that time that portion of what I saw ended. So I can't really explain that part any better than that. But I cannot emphasize how strong and black that power was.

You Will Not Experience My Wrath

"At this time I questioned the Lord, after this vision had ended; I said, 'Lord, are we going to have to go through this time with that black power I saw, and why did we have to go through a war? And is this the tribulation?' And the Lord came back to me in no uncertain terms, and He said: 'THERE IS A DIFFERENCE BETWEEN MY JUDGMENT AND MY WRATH. MY WRATH IS VENTED BECAUSE OF MY ANGER. YOU ARE IN THE WORLD BUT YOU ARE NOT OF THE WORLD, BUT YOU WILL HAVE TO GO THROUGH MY JUDGMENT WHEN I JUDGE THIS LAND, BUT YOU WILL NOT EXPERIENCE MY WRATH.' "

17
Persecuted Brethren

Nuclear war followed by a communist invasion would bring untold suffering to America, the Body of Christ included. Most American Christians would suffer for their lukewarmness, but a few brethren would suffer for their faith. The situation would be quite similar to that of Joshua and Caleb, who possessed the faith to enter Canaan, but because of their unbelieving brethren were also subjected to wandering through the wilderness under the judgment of God. But what made those forty years of wandering for Joshua and Caleb worthwhile was this: "For it is better, if it is the will of God, to suffer for doing good than for doing evil" (1 Pet. 3:17). Unfortunately, if communist troops ever encroach on our land, most Christians would fall into the latter category. However, during this time of judgment God will still endeavor, as He did with the Jews, to draw the Christians back to himself. If a believer, like Joshua or Caleb, ". . . suffers as a Christian, let him not be ashamed, but let him glorify God in this matter"

(1 Pet. 4:16). It is to these kind of believers that Peter wrote, "Therefore let those who suffer according to the will of God commit their souls to Him in doing good, as to a faithful Creator" (1 Pet. 4:19).

If God does judge America through communism, we shall soon join our brethren suffering under its rule. There is still time for America and the church to repent, but if they don't, be prepared for persecution. Do you love Jesus? I am convinced the Lord would have us know about this possible communist persecution ahead of time, so that if and when it does come we will know it is God's will to use it to turn the hearts of the American people towards himself.

The following prophecies describe American Christians who are persecuted for serving the Lord after a communist invasion of the United States.

Why So Many Soldiers?[22]

Evelyn Williams, a mother and street evangelist from Washington, D.C., dreamed of being persecuted by foreign troops for preaching the Gospel.

"In this one dream God gave me, I was ministering, I don't know where this place was, but I was in a big house with some friends of mine. My friend was in the service, and he was in charge of a battalion. I remember we were there that night preaching the Word, and people were getting saved and delivered. Then all of a sudden, in this dream I saw some soldiers who had come to their home. They had on little berets, and on their shoulders little sickles like a Nazi sign of some kind. It's wasn't an American sign. They weren't American soldiers. They all had rifles, and they lined the stairways of the house. And this couple was so upset and scared. From upstairs I saw them coming.

And there was a big clock on the wall. And they told the people to tell me, 'Tell her she better be gone by morning.' And there was something about quarter to six. This was the time I was supposed to leave. I don't know whether the daylight would have taken place at quarter to six, whether they could come and take me out at quarter to six. But I know at quarter to six something was going to happen. I had my plaid suitcase open, but I hadn't finished preaching the Word, and God didn't tell me what time to leave. My kids were standing there, and we were sort of frightened. We wanted to stay, yet something was telling us, 'You better leave.' Our friends were excited and sort of afraid too. But all I know was God said, 'You cannot leave because the work is not complete.' But these people were so angry. And I wondered, 'Why had so many of these soldiers come to get me?' These were the enemy, who had come to try and run us out; to try and take us over."

Kay Fowler's prophecy on American Christians after an invasion of America follows in three sections. The first part, "Green Meadow," depicts the initial invasion of America, and a place of refuge from the ensuing war. The second, "Deep in the Mountains," records the actual finding and living at Green Meadow. The third, "Passenger Train," portrays an effective Christian witness in the midst of adversity.

Green Meadow

"I saw at another time panic had hit our community, and that an invasion had come from the north. Everybody was in a frantic state. Above me were the darkest clouds I had ever seen. The cloud cover seemed to be for miles and miles; as far as I could see there was this dark storm cloud. Great fear seemed to come with the cloud, such fear that the cars were being driven off the highway, and the occupants would run out into the field. As I viewed all of this, I was given a map. There were no boundaries or states on it, so I know not what states or area this will be. But I could see each county was circled in black. And across each county was written 'Forbidden Zone.' And right in the center of this map of a particular county was written in green the words "Green Meadow." I knew this was my map, and that God was going to lead me out of all this war zone into this green meadow of His protection and safety. Now at this time I have no understanding to where these places might be. But I would that each of you put your trust in God and in the Spirit of Truth. For we have been given the Spirit of God as a comforter, and as a guide to lead us into all truth, and to keep us. As Jesus was telling His disciples the signs of His coming, He said, "Ye shall hear of wars and rumors of wars; see that ye be not troubled: for all these things must come to pass, but the end is not yet" (Matt. 24:6 KJV). Chapter 21, verses 18 and 19 of the book of Luke says, "But there shall not an hair of your head perish. In your patience possess ye your souls" (KJV).

Deep in the Mountains

"During the night hours I dreamed I was with a group of people. We had obtained a canvas-covered army truck, and were having to travel under cover of darkness so as not to be discovered by the soldiers that were already in the land. We were directed by an angel as he stood by the side of the road and pointed which road to take. We traveled a long way when we got to the foot of this mountain. The road that led to the top was just a narrow little pig trail. Now, I don't have the knowledge of the location of this area, but I do know that it was deep in the mountains. When we got to the top of this narrow road we found a forsaken campground, one that the soldiers had overlooked. At this campground there was running water, showers, and open grates for us to cook food on. As I was looking over the grounds, there before me I saw a giant clock that had come down from the sky, and it was superimposed over the ground. It had a hand on it that marked off sections; spring, summer, fall and winter. I saw the hand as it moved over each season. And at the end of the last season, I knew that we had been there a year. I looked at the base of the mountain, and the soldiers had discovered our tracks along the road. They were proceeding up the mountain when the dream ended. I know not what happened to us."

Passenger Train

"I've seen myself as a prisoner on a passenger train. There were others on this train. I don't know which country we were in, or where we were going. I'm standing before some of the prisoners, with an open Bible before me. I'm trying to teach them about Jesus, and tell them of His saving blood. A guard happened to walk through; I quickly hid the Bible behind my back, so I wouldn't be caught. After the guards have left, I bring the Bible back out and continue my teaching. I saw some Oriental faces among some of the people on this train."

Water-Tortured

Several years ago I had a dream and a vision concerning persecution of American Christians.

I heard in a dream the sound one would hear if he were to hit the end of a large steel drum with his fists. "Boom, boom, boom." The noise filled my entire being as if I were the drum. It was maddeningly insane. It was the most horrible experience I've ever had. The Lord then showed me the inside of my head. Don't ask me how, but as He did, the noise stopped. A beautiful quietness prevailed. I awoke from that dream and saw in a vision tiny drops of water dripping from a faucet about three feet from the ground onto my forehead. Immediately I knew I was being water-tortured. I also knew that by faith the Lord Jesus Christ would keep me from going insane. What a comfort that was.

The Time is Coming

While reading the Scriptures, I was impressed that the time is coming when American Christians will be martyred for their faith.

Jesus was talking to His disciples just before He went to the cross. "If the world hates you, you know that it hated Me before it hated you. . . . Remember the word that I said to you, 'A servant is not greater than his master.' If they persecuted Me, they will also persecute you. If they kept My word, they will keep yours also. But all these things they will do to you for My name's sake, because they do not know Him who sent Me" (John 15:18-21). "These things I have spoken to you, that you should not be made to stumble. They will put you out of the synagogues; yes, the time is coming that whoever kills you will think that he offers God service. And these things they will do to you because they have not known the Father nor Me" (John 16:1-3). Read through John 16:13.

The Lord has clearly shown me that martyrdom is going to take place in the church in America just as it did in the early church in Jerusalem. For a couple of years I was afraid to mention it to anyone. But now I know I must.

18
Revival

Down through the centuries God has brought revival to a desperate world through His Church. When all seemed lost, when all hope has been gone, when men wrung their hands in disgust and hung their heads in despair, the Church, time and time again, has risen to the occasion and significantly changed the course of history. Nineveh, Israel, England, America and many other parts of the globe have experienced tremendous ourpourings of God's Spirit that have dramatically transformed the framework and fabric of those societies for many future generations.

Jerusalem. After the seventy-year Babylonian captivity, a remnant of Israel's southern kingdom not only returned to the land, but also to the Lord. They rebuilt Jerusalem and worshiped God (Ezra 1-6). The returning captives experienced great revival.

The prophet Zechariah vividly described the southern kingdom's restoration. "Thus says the Lord: I am returning to Jerusalem with mercy; My house shall be built in it, says the Lord of hosts . . . My cities shall again spread out through prosperity; the Lord will again comfort Zion, and will again choose Jerusalem. . . . Old men and old women shall again sit in the streets of Jerusalem, each one with his staff in his hand because of great age. The streets of the city shall be full of boys and girls playing in its streets" (Zech. 1:16, 17; 8:4, 5).

America's great heritage has been built by those men and women who dared to believe God for revival. Reverend Owen Murphy in his booklet "When God Stepped Down From Heaven" described the effect revival had upon our nation, particularly New England, just prior to the Civil War:

The American Revival of 1857

The mighty "visitation" of those days, from which has flowed almost a century of spiritual blessing, represents a challenge, even today. Like a spiritual tornado, the Spirit of God swept through the land, and New England became the center of the great awakening, resulting in great numbers finding Salvation. In some towns it was reported as being "almost impossible to find anyone who had not been converted." Like a great spiritual epidemic, tremendous CONVICTION OF SIN swept through the land, and thousands turned to Christ. Drunkards, as they stood at the saloon bars, gamblers as they sat at the card tables, congregations as they sat in churches, even passengers on board incoming liners came under the influence of this strange and wonderful moving of God and, kneeling in repentance found pardon.

In many places, dancehalls, theatres, and gambling dens were closed or emptied; new churches began to spring up everywhere; family altars were restored, and the spirit of prayer grew in intensity until anyone could cross the land and find a "mid-day" prayer meeting in almost any town! It was estimated, that as many as 50,000 decisions were made in a week, when this gracious visitation was at its height! Following in its wake came mighty preachers of the Word of God, including D.L. Moody, under whose ministry multitudes were called to repentance; and pioneer missionaries who have taken the gospel to the uttermost parts of the earth.

The Hebrides Revival

Perhaps the greatest revival in recent times took place between 1949 and 1952 in the Hebrides, a sparsely populated small group of islands off the coast of Scotland. Two elderly sisters had prayed for years, and a number of men had met three nights a week for five months in a barn for all-night prayer meetings until revival swept the islands like a mighty rushing wind.

In his pamphlet *When God Stepped Down From Heaven* Owen Murphy recounted the supernatural scenes that transpired there.

Buses came from the four corners of the island, crowding the church. Seven men were being driven to the meeting in a butcher's truck, when suddenly the Spirit of God fell upon them in great conviction, and all were converted before they reached the church! As the preacher delivered his message, tremendous conviction of sin swept down upon the people! Tears rolled down the faces of the people, and from every part of the building came cries of men and women crying for mercy. So deep was the distress of some that their voices could be heard outside in the road. A young man beneath the pulpit cried out: *"O God, hell is too good for me!"*

The meeting closed with the Benediction and the people began to move out. As the last person was about to leave, a young man began to pray. Under a tremendous burden of intercession, he prayed for three quarters of an hour and, as he prayed, the people kept gathering until there were twice as many outside the church as there were inside! When the young man stopped praying, the Elder gave out Psalm 132, and as the great congregation sang the old hymn, the people streamed back into the church again, and the meeting went on until 4 A.M.

The moment people took their seats, the Spirit of God in awful conviction began to sweep through the church, and hardened sinners began to weep and confess their sins.

Just as the meeting was closing, a messenger hurried up to the preacher, very excited:

"COME WITH ME! THERE'S A CROWD OF PEOPLE OUTSIDE THE POLICE STATION; THEY ARE WEEPING AND IN AWFUL DISTRESS. WE DON'T KNOW WHAT'S WRONG WITH THEM, BUT THEY ARE CALLING FOR SOMEONE TO COME AND PRAY WITH THEM!"

Describing the scenes outside the police station, which reminded one of the amazing days of Charles Finney, and the Welsh Revival, the minister declared:

"I SAW A SIGHT I NEVER THOUGHT WAS POSSIBLE. SOMETHING I SHALL NEVER FORGET. UNDER A STARLIT SKY, MEN AND WOMEN WERE KNEELING EVERYWHERE, BY THE ROADSIDE,

OUTSIDE THE COTTAGES, EVEN BEHIND THE PEAT STACKS, CRYING FOR GOD TO HAVE MERCY UPON THEM!"

Nearly 600 people, who had been making their way to the church, when suddenly the Spirit of God had fallen upon them in great conviction—like Paul on the way to Damascus—causing them to fall to their knees in repentance!

REVIVAL HAD SURELY COME! For five weeks it swept on in that one Parish, Duncan Campbell conducted four services nightly; in one church at 7 o'clock, in another at 10, in a third at midnight, and back to the first one at 3 o'clock, and home between 5 and 6 o'clock—tired, but very happy to be in the midst of such a wonderful moving of God.

After five weeks in this district the revival began to spread and what had taken place in Barvas, was repeated in other districts.

As men and women throughotu the island began to grip God in desperate intercession and prayer for revival, the Spirit of God swept on in increasing power.

THEN a small community, came within the path of this spiritual tornado. Gripped by a spirit of religious indifference, it was reckoned that hardly a young person darkened the House of God; the Sabbath being given over to the drinking house, poaching, and other sinful pleasures. News of the gracious moving of God having spread through the island, it was here where an opposition meeting was held, lest a similar visitation fall upon Arnol. Although the church was crowded with those who came from the various parts of the island, very few people from Arnol attended the services. In desperation, the little prayer band made their way to the farmhouse to plead the promises of God. Just after midnight, a young man rose to his feet and prayed a prayer that will never be forgotten by those who were present.

"LORD, YOU MADE A PROMISE, ARE YOU GOING TO FULFILL IT? WE BELIEVE THAT YOU ARE A COVENANT KEEPING GOD. WILL YOU BE TRUE TO YOUR COVENANT? YOU HAVE SAID THAT YOU WILL POUR WATER UPON HIM THAT IS THIRSTY AND FLOODS UPON THE DRY GROUND. LORD, I DO NOT KNOW HOW THESE MINISTERS STAND IN YOUR PRESENCE, BUT IF I KNOW MY OWN HEART I KNOW WHERE I STAND, AND I TELL THEE NOW THAT I AM THIRSTY. OH, I AM THIRSTY FOR A MANIFESTATION OF THE PRESENCE AND POWER OF GOD! AND "LORD, BEFORE I SIT DOWN, I WANT TO TELL YOU THAT YOUR HONOUR IS AT STAKE!"

(Have you ever prayed like that? Here is a man praying the prayer of faith that Heaven must answer! One could imagine the angels of Heaven looking over the battlements of Glory and saying: "This is a man who believes God! This is a man who dares to stand firm upon the promise of God and take from God what has been promised!")

Then came the answer! There are those in Arnol today who will verify the fact that while the brother prayed the house shook like a leaf (just as in Acts 4) as God turned loose His mighty power! Dishes rattled upon the sideboard; an elder exclaimed: "An earth tremor?" Then wave after wave of Divine Power swept through the room. *Simultaneously, the Spirit of God swept through the village. PEOPLE COULD NOT SLEEP; HOUSES WERE LIT ALL NIGHT; PEOPLE*

WALKED THE STREETS IN GREAT CONVICTION; OTHERS KNELT BY THEIR BEDSIDES CRYING FOR GOD TO PARDON THEM! As the praying men left the prayer meeting, the preacher walked into a house for a glass of milk and found the lady of the house, with seven others, down upon their knees, crying for pardon. *Within 48 hours the drinking house, usually crowded with the drinking men of the village, was closed. Today, it is in ruins. Fourteen young men who had been drinking there, were gloriously converted. Those same men could be found three times a week, with others, down upon their knees before God, from 10 o'clock until after midnight, praying for their old associates and the spread of revival.* It was in this village that within 48 hours nearly every young person between the ages of 12 and 20 had surrendered to Christ, and it was reckoned that every young man between the ages of 18 and 35 could be found in the prayer meetings!

In BERNERAY, things were very difficult as the stream of religious life was very low; churches were empty and prayer meetings were practically nil. In view of this, a wire was sent to the praying men of Barvas to come and assist in prayer, and bring with them Donald Smith, the 17-year-old boy to whom God had imparted the amazing ministry of prayer. Halfway through his message, the preacher stopped, and called out *"DONALD WILL YOU LEAD US IN PRAYER!"* Standing to his feet, he began to pour out his heart before God in agonizing intercession for the people of the island, and reminding God that He was the great "Covenant-keeping God." Suddenly, it seemed as though the heavens were rent and God swept into the church. People everywhere were stricken by the

Power of God, as the Spirit swept through in great convicting power. Outside, startling things were taking place. *Simultaneously the Spirit of God had swept over the homes and area around the village, and everywhere people came under great conviction of sin. Fishermen out in their boats, men behind their looms, men at the pit bank, a merchant out with his truck, school teachers examining their papers, were gripped by God and by 10 o'clock the roads were black with people, streaming from every direction to the church.* As the preacher came out of the church, the Spirit of God swept in among the people on the road, as a wind. They gripped each other in fear. In agony of soul they trembled, many wept and some fell to the ground in great conviction of sin. Three men were found lying by the side of the road in such distress of soul that they could not even speak—*yet they had never been near the church!*

So tremendous was the supernatural moving of God in conviction of sin, not a home, not a family, not an individual escaped fearful conviction, and even the routine of business was stopped that the island might seek the Face of God like Nineveh of Bible days.

After a service in Keswick, England relating the moving of God's Spirit in the Hebrides, Brother Murphy was prophetically exhorted by Duncan Campbell:

> When you return to America, rouse the people; tell them what God is doing! I believe every church can have what we are having in the Hebrides. There is no "mystery," but there is a "secret." If God can find a people

over there, prepared to "pay the price" as they have over here, He will visit them in the same revival of power!

Owen Murphy described his reaction to this dynamic challenge:

> Every word that fell from his lips seemed to burn into my soul, as I became conscious that the Spirit of God was speaking to me, and giving me a new commission. As I remembered the tremendous impact of the message upon that great crowd of people that afternoon, a great conviction gripped me— Here was the message of the hour which surely every minister and church ought to hear! Cancelling my evangelistic campaigns, I returned immediately to AMERICA to rouse the people to seek the Face of God that a similar spiritual awakening might speedily be given.

Thanks to brother Murphy and others, America has periodically experienced small outbreaks of revival over the past three decades. But God still yearns to pour out His Spirit in such magnitude that the entire nation will be affected, as in the Hebrides. The church must first "pay the price." The cost of revival is great, but the cost of judgment is greater.

Backslidden Nations and Churches. There have always been small pockets of revival even in the most backslidden of nations. As evil as Israel was during the time Ahab and Jezebel ruled their land, there were, much to Elijah's surprise, 7,000 Israelites who had not bowed their knee to Baal (1 Kings 19:18). The same can be said of churches. The Holy Spirit spoke to the Church at Sardis, "You have a few names even in Sardis who have not defiled their garments" (Rev. 3:4).

There are times of spiritual refreshment, of explosive evangelism, of real revival for American Christians today, just as there were for the numerous Hebrides believers, as well as the faithful few in Sardis. American Christians can also participate in a heaven-sent Holy Spirit-anointed revival that would affect the whole nation for God. Please note: at this time God wills to revive and use the entire Christian Church in America for His purposes, not just a faithful few.

America's Next Revival

The first two segments of George Washington's prophetic vision have come to pass, and if there isn't a deep repentance throughout the Christian Church and the nation as a whole, the third part will soon be fulfilled. But even so, according to Washington's vision, America will rise again. Its sovereignty will be restored for as long as "the stars remain, and the heaven send down dew upon the earth." In light of Washington's vision America will have revival; if not before a nuclear strike and foreign invasion, then certainly after. However, God's will for the Church and the nation at the time of writing this book is *repentance preceding revival—now!*

God Desires Revival. America's next revival must begin in the life of each and every American Christian. If it does not start here it will never happen. Often I have prayed and fasted, as many of you have done, for God to send revival to America, and to the rest of the world as well. And recently, as I was interceding for this to occur, I entered the throne room of heaven with my request. (In heaven, communication is instant. The Lord not only heard my plea, but immediately discerned the intent of my spirit. Even more profound was the knowledge that I could instantly perceive that the Lord had comprehended the attitude of my heart.) And the Word of the Lord came to me from the direction of the throne saying, "I will not send revival"—and then He paused—"but I will bring revival through you."

Up until this time I had thought revival to be a sovereign supernatural work performed solely by the Holy Spirit. Suddenly I realized God had desired *my entire being* to become a vessel, a channel through which His revival would come to this world, particularly America. The more I pondered this truth, the more sense it made. There could not have been thousands added to the church in Jerusalem without the 120 dedicated believers in the upper room (Acts 1-2). There would not have been any conversions in Samaria, either, if Philip the evangelist and later the apostles John and Peter had not been willing to go there (Acts 8:4-25). And wherever the apostle Paul went, revival went too! In each generation God has brought revival to various parts of the globe through members of His Church who were willing to commit their all. God wills to do the exact same thing through His Church (you and I) in America today.

Don't Give Up On America

The late Jesse Winley (1920-1980), street preacher, church evangelist, and bishop of the Soul Saving Station in the Harlem section of New York City, foresaw a tremendous revival taking place in America.

"Revival is coming to America. God revealed this to me. Jesus Christ appeared to me. He told me to get up, and God the Father spoke. He said, 'Do you realize what you have in your hand?' I had the Bible. God said, 'That's My Word.' When He spoke it seemed to echo throughout eternity. He said, 'Take it out and throw it.' I took the Bible and threw it, and by the time it hit the ground it had turned into a container like an old movie reel. Then it turned to molten lava. I was in the deep part of the South, and that lava spread across the state of Florida, then Georgia and all the border states, and up through Washington, D.C., Delaware and New Jersey. Everywhere it went men were running and screaming; multitudes were crying for mercy. It was God's convicting power. It came up through New York, and on to Massachusetts. It covered the whole Province of Nova Scotia, Canada and it went on out to the sea. God said, 'Don't give up on America. I'm going to pour out My spirit on all flesh. The multitudes of sinners are not going to be lost.' "

Glory Cloud

While teaching a series on the restoration of David's Tabernacle during a 1972 World Map camp at Warm Beach, Washington, a minister from New Zealand beheld a vision of a glorious white cloud that arose over the northwestern United States. The cloud spread across our nation dispelling a black cloud that had risen over the northeast and had endeavored to envelop our land.

"I see a [black] cloud arising on the east coast of the United States, and it is spreading across the northeastern section. This black cloud is arising from a spot (I do not know America) but all I can say is it is in the north and in the east over by the sea. This very black, murky cloud is trying to sweep westward and southward. I can see in the northwest of America another cloud arising, and this cloud is white. This cloud, because of its brightness, is shining out many glorious, radiant colors. I see there is a conflict between this black, grey, brown, murky cloud and this beautiful, shining, radiant cloud which is rising up. . . . But . . . the black cloud is being overshadowed . . . by the power of the brightness of [the white] cloud. And now the cloud from the northwest is moving speedily southwestward and eastward, and from underneath it rain is beginning to fall. The color of this rain is pure white. It is raining, but it looks like snow. . . . Small pools of water are beginning to form on the ground. These pools are also like the color of the cloud—white, radiant and sparkling. Small rivers and streams are beginning to flow from each little lake. . . . The rivers, the lakes and more and more of the land mass of America is being covered by this beautiful sparkling water. . . . And not only is America being covered by this beautiful, white, radiant water, but now I see the vision is going further away and I'm beginning to see many other nations of the world."

As the vision concluded the minister was given a prophecy pertaining to the vision's interpretation.

"For behold there are those in these days who would plot, fight, and scheme against thee, who would endeavor to break down the very structure on which thy nation is built. But I say unto thee that the cloud has already risen; that's the Spirit. And behold the cloud that I shall send is a pure cloud dropping pure rain upon pure hearts. And the rivers which I shall send as a result of the rain that shall fall from the cloud no man shall be able to stop, and no weapon formed against thee shall prosper. For I have purposed in My heart, saith God, to revive and refresh, as never before, this nation; and to make you a blessing unto many nations."

Author's note: The black cloud the minister saw arising from a spot on the northeast coast is a hole in the spirit world emanating demonic powers. Satan has concentrated much of his efforts to destroy the United States in the northeast because it is the bedrock of our nation's Christian heritage.

I Give You the Land

En route from Portland, Oregon to the 1980 Washington (D.C.) for Jesus rally I realized that God wills His Church to bring revival to America. I was behind the wheel of a car traveling through the very heartland of America. Two other brethren who had shared the rigors of driving all night were fast asleep. The morning sun revealed endless fields of golden spring wheat stretching out to the horizons and beyond. As I viewed this great expanse, God spoke to my spirit: "Everywhere the soul of your foot shall tread I have given it unto you. I give you the land!" As I quickly glanced at the magnificent panorama surrounding me I distinctly remember briefly lifting my eyes heavenward and confidently yet humbly saying, "Lord, as a member of Your Body, everywhere the wheel of this Torino rolls I claim it for Your glory." I felt like Joshuah or Caleb entering Canaan, or like a Pilgrim standing on Plymouth Rock. Oh, the joy of believing God!

Brethren, God has given us this land. It is ours. Let us go forth at once and possess it for the glory of our

God and His Christ. The Holy Spirit is moving in God's people. An ever increasing number of American Christians are catching the vision for revival. In central New Jersey, eastern Massachusetts and Portland, Oregon, pastors are gathering together for the purpose of revival. Throughout America there are many more pastors, Christian ministers, and members of the Body of Christ who regardless of the cost are committed to seeing revival sweep through their locality along with the rest of the nation.

It is possible that revival will not transform America until God's judgments have driven the church to her knees. Some prophecies have foreseen revival happening in the midst of judgment. The conclusion of the Statue of Liberty vision seen in 1954 portrayed the condition of the saints during the time when deadly vapors and nuclear blasts would engulf America and other parts of the world.

"And then to my ears came another sound—a sound of distant singing. It was the sweetest music I had ever heard. There was joyful shouting, and sounds of happy laughter. Immediately I knew it was the rejoicing of the saints of God. I looked, and there high in the heaven, above the smoke and poisonous gases, above the noise of battle, I saw a huge mountain. It seemed to be of solid rock, and I knew at once that this was the mountain of the Lord. The sounds of music and rejoicing were coming from a cleft, high up in the side of the rock mountain.

"It was the saints of God who were doing the rejoicing. It was God's own people who were singing and dancing and shouting with joy, safe from all the harm which had come upon the earth, for they were hidden away in the cleft of the rock. There in the cleft, they were shut in, protected by a great, giant hand which reached out of the heavens, and which was none other than the hand of God, shutting them in until the storm was over—passed."

In 1961, the missionary from Haiti (who had confirmed brother Lambert's vision, on page 135, of great and terrible judgments coming upon the earth) beheld a similar vision, and saw that "the saints were hidden during this time, but the Spirit-led saints were walking around viewing all this terrible confusion, death, and weeping. The people that were tormented asked why the Spirit-led saints were not affected by all this trouble, and they said it was because they were led by the Lord, and He had overcome the world, and that they too had overcome the world through Him."

John Jackson's prophetic account of revival coming forth in America during a time of judgment is joyful yet sobering.

Persecution and Denial[22]

Jackson testified, "The Lord showed me two words: persecution and denial. And I saw men denying the Lord. People would come to them and say, 'You're a Christian, aren't you?' and they would say, 'Oh, no, I used to be but I saw the error in that way, and I am through with that movement.' And then I also saw them that night going home and saying, 'God I'm sorry, I was weak, I was weak before You, I am sorry,' and being remorseful in their beings and hurt deeply by that.

"I saw this as a time when God will miraculously provide. He will provide farms. He will provide water. He will provide food. Food will appear on tables without any preparation of the food because faith will come. People will say, 'Lord, You have promised You will provide; let's pray!' I saw a family pray, and when they prayed the prayer of faith and opened their eyes, there was food on that table. That is how God will provide for those who are strong in Him. But if we deny Him, what can we expect God to do for us? We have to be strong.

"I've likened it to being able to run a four-minute spiritual mile. It takes years of practice to run a four-minute mile. And it will take us years of working and growing in the Lord to run a four-minute spiritual mile. Brother Thomas, if I could convey any more the victory that I have seen throughout all these in Jesus Christ, I would. But I am at a loss for words . . ."

Conclusion

The Scriptures, historical records and the prophetic Word all point to the fact that America's future is held primarily in the hands of the Christians. And in spite of drug, alcohol, marital, moral and other sundry problems, it is the American church of believers, who belong to numerous Christian denominations and independent Christian churches, who will determine the destiny of America. Regardless of our eschatological positions, if we are honest before God, we ought to acknowledge that we Christians are the paramount cause for God sending judgment upon America. But we can also be the main reason America experiences revival and is restored. *The choice is ours.*

Whatever It Takes. God is going to have His way in America because His people in America are going to want His way. We shall desire that God will use us to bring to America a revival equivalent to the day of Pentecost, a revival where saints are in "one accord" and sinners are "cut to the heart" (Acts 2:1, 37). Whatever it takes, God will accomplish His plan and purpose in and through His church. Unfortunately, I fear that the American Body of Christ will have to learn the hard way. God does not desire America to be bombed and invaded by Russia and other communist countries. Though God is saying this *will* happen if we Christians do not repent, that does not mean He *wants* it to come upon us. The Lord was grieved over the thought of the Babylonians conquering Judah: "My eyes will weep bitterly and run down with tears, because the Lord's flock has been taken captive" (Jer. 13:17). Likewise, Jesus wept over Jerusalem knowing the gentiles (Romans) would destroy the city (Luke 19:41-44).

Although it hurt Him deeply, God, in His love, engineered those judgments not only as a chastisement for sins but also as a means of restoring the nation of Israel to a right relationship with himself (Lev. 26:27-45, Luke 21:20-24). God wanted His people in Israel then, as He does His people in America today, to be effective witnesses of His glory to the unsaved, "among whom you shine as lights in this world" (Phil. 2:15).

The Word of the Lord. One day as I finished preaching on a street corner the message of God sending cataclysmic judgments upon America to overthrow it, and calling people, especially Christians, to repentance, the Lord spoke a prophetic word through me saying, "This is how you will know the word of the Lord. If you hear a word and that word comes to pass, then you will know that the Lord has spoken this word."

The majority of people, including Christians, who

read this book may not believe its message until after the fact. When the Lord, through the prophet Habakkuk, informed Judah of a future Babylonian invasion, He exclaimed: "Look among the nations and watch—be utterly astounded! For I will work a work in your days which you would not believe, though it were told you" (Hab. 1:5). Granted, some will acknowledge the validity of coming judgment and their need of repentance, but mere mental assent is not true Bible belief. We must act upon what we know to be true. Otherwise we don't truly believe.

I am totally convinced God's will for America today is revival preceded by repentance. However, what God wants us to do (rid ourselves of lukewarmness and withdraw from the WCC) and what we shall do are two different stories. I remind you that we are entering "the throes of judgment," the time of "the third great peril." With each passing day the likelihood of repentance in the church and nation prior to the arrival of the judgments in this book becomes increasingly less.

Jeremiah Stops Praying. America's present situation is comparable to Jerusalem's just before the Babylonian invasion in 586 B.C. For nearly two hundred years the Lord had sent prophet after prophet to warn, exhort, and encourage the inhabitants of Jerusalem to repent of their sins and return to God, lest foreign invaders ravage the city (Jer. 7:25-27). And even though most of the nation of Israel (the ten northern tribes and a good portion of Judah) had already been conquered, repentance was still the will of God for Jerusalem right up until three years before the Babylonian invasion when the Lord instructed Jeremiah: "Do not pray for this people, for their good. . . . I will consume them by the sword, by the famine, and by the pestilence" (Jer. 14:11, 12). Proof of this is found in Jeremiah 18:11, 12 where the Lord's next and final call to repentance was immediately rejected by the people. America has not crossed this bridge, but is moving dangerously closer.

Isaiah's Prophecy. Amazing as it may seem, one hundred fifty years prior to the fall of Jerusalem the prophet Isaiah not only predicted the conquest of the entire nation, but also its return to the Promised Land from captivity (Isa. 44:21-28). However, if either Jerusalem, Judah, or the ten northern tribes had chosen to obey the Word of the Lord spoken by the prophets, then God would have restored the nation of Israel without the use of foreign conquerors. God offered the Jewish people Plan A: Repentance and Revival. They refused it. Therefore, in His mercy, God instituted Plan B: Judgment, Repentance and Revival. They finally responded in faith.

If America, particularly the Church, does not repent, then foreign communist troops will invade our land subsequent to a limited nuclear first strike by the Soviet Union. If we repent, then our nation will be spared. But if the former be true, surely God's chastening hand of love will then persuade His people in America to humble themselves before Him while at the same time drawing many unbelievers to himself. And the prophetic word contained in this book, as well as the prophetic words spoken and written by other brethren who carry this message, will not only be remembered but will also have a profound effect upon and be received by those who had previously read or heard them as the Word of the Lord.

I am sure the same could have been said for the Jews who remembered the words of Isaiah and the other prophets while the enemy was in their land or while they were in captivity.

Let us once again ponder the words of the father of our country, George Washington. "The shadowy angel for the last time dipped water from the ocean and sprinkled it upon America. Instantly the dark cloud rolled back, together with the armies it had brought, leaving the inhabitants of the land victorious.

"Then once more, I beheld the villages, towns and cities springing up where I had seen them before, while the bright angel, planting the azure Standard he had brought in the midst of them, cried with a loud voice: 'While the stars remain, and the heaven send down dew upon the earth, so long shall the Union last.' And taking from his brow the crown on which blazoned the word 'Union,' he placed it upon the Standard while the people, kneeling down said, 'Amen.'"

Brethren, we do not have to wait until thermonuclear warheads devastate our cities, until foreign troops pummel our land, until we are herded into concentration camps or loaded into ships and exported as slaves before we bow our knees unto our God and say "Amen." We can turn to the Lord in repentance *now*. In times past, has not God's hand of judgment been stayed when His people have repented, fasted and prayed? Judgment can be avoided if we obey the Lord.

Although America is facing imminent judgment, God is still calling American Christians to repent of their lukewarmness and to sever their ties with the WCC. God is not sitting around waiting to send judgment. But because of His great love He continues, as He once did with Israel of old, to mercifully strive by warning us of coming judgment in hope that we will turn from our sins and accept His will for our lives.

Not only does God wish us to repent; He wants to include you and me in His plan for revival in America. Revival, not judgment, is God's will for America. Because it is God's will, we can have revival in our lives, homes, churches and nation. America does not have to be overthrown in judgment, and the church severely chastised. God longs to be merciful and to relent of His judgments. If you and I will hear His voice and not harden our hearts (Heb. 4:7); if you and I will humble ourselves and pray, and seek His face and turn from our wicked ways, then God will hear from heaven. He will pardon our iniquity! He will spare us! God will bring revival through us, and by that means heal our land (2 Chron. 7:14). Alleluia!

I trust that by having read this book God's burden for this nation and His Church has been birthed in your heart by the realization of God's merciful attitude and compassionate behavior towards those who deserve His judgment.

God bless you.

The author welcomes correspondence. Please write to:

Revival Center
P.O. Box 4042
Warren, NJ 07060

Footnotes to Part 4

1. Charles R. Taylor, *World War III and the Destiny of America* (Nashville: Thomas Nelson Publishers, 1979).
2. David Wilkerson, *Set the Trumpet to Thy Mouth* (Lindale, Texas: World Challenge, Inc., 1985), pp. 1, 10.
3. From *God Speaks Today*, edited by Gerald Derstine, originally printed in *Harvest Time*, May-June 1964.
4. Reprinted with permission of United Press International, Inc.
5. Ibid.
6. *U.S. News and World Report*, Aug. 8, 1983, p. 8.
7. Harry Genet, "WCC: A Case of Indigestion," *Christianity Today*, Feb. 2, 1979, p. 89.
8. Editorial, "The WCC Finances Violence to Combat Racism," *Christianity Today*, Nov. 20, 1981, p. 20.
9. Ibid.
10. "Potter Power," *Time Magazine*, Jan. 22, 1979, p. 72.
11. Richard M. Ostling, "The Curious Politics of Ecumenism," *Time Magazine*, Aug. 22, 1983, p. 46.
12. Kenneth I. Woodward, "The Road to Christian Unity," *Newsweek*, Aug. 22, 1983, p. 41.
13. "Churchmen Mum About Soviet Sins," *U.S. News & World Report*, Aug. 22, 1983, p. 9.
14. Leonard Ravenhill, *American Is Too Young To Die* (Minneapolis: Bethany Fellowship, 1979), p. 121.
15. W.C. Moore, "The Gates of Hell Shall Not Prevail," *Herald of His Coming*, 1982.

16. "Where Are the Volunteers for God's Army of Prayer Warriors?", *Herald of His Coming,* 1984.
17. Norman Grubb, *Rees Howells Intercessor* (Fort Washington, PA: Christian Literature Crusade, 1983), p. 261.
18. Ibid., p. 262.
19. Adela Rogers St. Johns, *Tell No Man* (Garden City, NY: Doubleday, 1966), p. 29.
20. Taylor, op. cit.
21. Transcribed from an interview on KVTT radio, Dallas, TX, 1981.
22. Transcribed from a telephone conversation.
23. Frank Bartleman, *Azusa Street* (South Plainfield, NJ: Bridge Publishing, Inc., 1980), p. 54.